CORETTA

CORETTA

The Story of Coretta Scott King

COMMEMORATIVE EDITION

Octavia Vivian

FORTRESS PRESS
Minneapolis

CORETTA
The Story of Coretta Scott King
Commemorative Edition

Cover art: Coretta Scott King speaks at a news conference in 1985. (AP
  Photo)
Frontispiece: Coretta Scott King is shown during an interview at the
  Martin Luther King Jr. Center for Social Change in Atlanta, January
  1975. (AP Photo/Joe Holloway)
Cover and interior design: James Korsmo

ISBN-13: 978-0-8006-3855-9 (hc)
ISBN-10: 0-8006-3855-7 (hc)
ISBN-13: 978-0-8006-3853-5 (pb)
ISBN-10: 0-8006-3853-0 (pb)

The paper used in this publication meets the minimum requirements of
American National Standard for Information Sciences—Permanence of
Paper for Printed Library Materials, ANSI Z329.48-1984.

Manufactured in the U.S.A.

09   08   07   06   1   2   3   4   5   6   7   8   9   10

Dedicated to
MRS. CHRISTINE KING FARRIS

For your unfailing love of Coretta Scott King.
For sharing your most fragile and intimate
thoughts, ideas, and memories of her.
Your friendship and dedication to her painted
the perfect picture of sisterhood, both in life and in Christ.
That bond has been the catalyst and inspiration
for the revision of this book.
So to you I say, thank you.

CONTENTS

Contents

FOREWORD

Martin Luther King III

So many of the books about the American Civil Rights Movement and its leaders have been written by people who were not involved in our freedom struggle. Not surprisingly, these works often miss the mark in terms of accuracy, focus, and interpretation. I am always encouraged, therefore, when movement insiders write books that illuminate our freedom movement and the leaders who made it such a historic success. Such a book is *Coretta* by Octavia Vivian, who was herself a dear friend of my mother, Coretta Scott King, and a strong, actively involved supporter of the American Civil Rights Movement.

Octavia Vivian brings the special empathy of shared experience to this unique biography of my mother. Like Coretta Scott King, Octavia Vivian was an activist in her own right. She was one of the participants in the Nashville sit-ins and one of the first to eat in a downtown department store restaurant. Like Coretta Scott King, she was also the wife, partner, and coworker of a heroic leader of the Civil Rights Movement—in her case, the Reverend C. T. Vivian. And like my mother, she too was the mother of a houseful of active, energetic children while making her unique contribution to freedom and equality in America.

The book you hold in your hands is an extraordinarily insightful and perceptive account of the life of my mother,

Coretta Scott King, a great American woman who was honored and celebrated all over the world and who did more than any other individual to educate the world about the life, work, and teachings of Martin Luther King, Jr. The dramatic and uplifting story of her life is beautifully evoked in these pages—her roots and childhood, the education that prepared her for leadership, her historic partnership with Martin Luther King, Jr., her family life, her courageous, visionary leadership in the years after his assassination, and the many other contributions that gave hope and inspiration to so many.

PREFACE

The idea for a book about Mrs. Martin Luther King, Jr.—Coretta—was first conceived as a tribute to a powerful woman behind a great man. Her husband read the early pages of the first edition of this book and was considering writing an introduction. Now, in this commemorative edition, I have updated and augmented the original book to take account of Coretta's momentous accomplishments since the assassination of her husband. These pages have become an assessment of a woman with a commitment that remained unwavering in spite of the loss of her husband and decades of labor for his cause. There still stands a determination to carry the work of the Civil Rights Movement to its ultimate end—a Human Rights Movement.

I have relied here on materials collected from Mrs. King's articles, speeches, and musical performances. Additional information came from conversations with Mrs. King; Mrs. King's mother, Mrs. Bernice Scott; Russell Goode of Chattanooga, Tennessee, who served as Mrs. King's accompanist; numerous Civil Rights workers; and from my own recollections. In both editions I have drawn heavily from many newspaper and magazine articles, Lerone Bennett's book, *What Manner of Man*, and Dr. King's books *Stride toward Freedom* and *Why We Can't Wait*, as well as Coretta's own *My Life with Martin Luther King, Jr.*

I am fondly indebted to the late Ed Clayton, author of a children's book about Dr. King, *A Peaceful Warrior.* Prior to his death in late 1966, Ed encouraged me greatly when I told him I wanted to write a book about Mrs. King. A reading by Mrs. Pamela Morton also proved invaluable to me.

I am indebted to my six children, Alvier Denise, Cordy Jr., Kira, Mark, Anita Charisse, and Albert, whose good behavior at the time of the first writing afforded their mother time to write; and to my stepdaughter Jo Anna Walker for her vote of confidence. And most of all, to my husband, the Reverend C. T. Vivian, whose dedication to God, country, and the nonviolent protest movement eventually led him to the executive staff of Dr. King's Southern Christian Leadership Conference. It was through C. T. that I first met Coretta.

Throughout the wonderful journey of re-creating this book, many people helped me make my vision a reality. I would like to thank my three daughters, Denise Morse, Kira Holden, and Charisse Thornton; and my two daughters-in-law, Utrophia Vivian and DeAna Jo Vivian. All of them have supported me greatly, whether they were typing or helping me give birth to my thoughts. I appreciate each of you for your time, patience, energy, faith, and diligence, but most of all for caring about me. I would also like to thank Asia Myles for her creative editing expertise and for her patience and understanding. Without the love and support from you all, this book would not have been possible.

CHAPTER I

HOMEGOING

The nation awakened to the news that Coretta Scott King had died quietly in her sleep at an alternative medical clinic in Mexico on January 30, 2006, at 2:00 A.M. Since both of her parents died in their nineties, it was hard to believe that Coretta was dead at seventy-eight years of age. Although just months earlier she had suffered a stroke, most were optimistic. The public was not aware that she was also battling ovarian cancer. Just three weeks prior to her passing, she attended the King Center's annual "Salute to Greatness" dinner, and although she was not able to speak she received a roaring standing ovation.

Throughout the world, there was much disbelief that our "First Lady" had passed. Before Coretta's body returned to the States, many people throughout the country brought flowers, shed tears, and recited prayers at the tomb of Dr. Martin Luther King, Jr.

Upon hearing the news of Coretta King's death, Georgia's governor, Sonny Perdue, ordered the state Capitol flag to be flown at half-mast. He also invited the King family to have

Coretta lie in state under the Georgia Capitol dome. Due to the prejudices and traditions of the South during the 1960s, Governor Lester Maddox denied such an honor to Dr. Martin Luther King, Jr. On February 4, 2006, Coretta King was the twenty-first person to lie in state at the Georgia State Capitol. She was the first African American and the first woman so honored. Unlike the mule-drawn wagon that transported the casket of Dr. Martin Luther King, Jr., Coretta's casket was transported through the city of Atlanta in a horse-drawn carriage.

After leaving the Willie A. Watkins Funeral Home, Coretta's casket traveled down Martin Luther King Drive until it reached the west entrance of the Capitol. Thousands of people lined the streets while thousands more watched via television to pay their respects and get a glimpse of history. When Coretta's carriage reached the Capitol, Georgia State Patrol officers carried the casket into the rotunda where the governor's private memorial was held. Coretta was dressed in a beautiful pink pantsuit. The casket was adorned with white and colored roses. City and state officials, Coretta's family, close friends and many Civil Rights leaders paid their respects. Although the public viewing was scheduled to begin at noon, a line began to form at the Georgia Capitol at 6:30 A.M. By the end of the day, an estimated 42,000 public viewers stood in the cold and windy weather to pay their respects to Coretta Scott King.

On Monday, February 6, a second public viewing was held at Ebenezer Baptist Church. The third public viewing was held on Tuesday, February 7, at New Birth Baptist Church in Lithonia, Georgia. In three days, there were an estimated 170,000 public viewers. Many stood in line for hours in the late night and early morning while battling the cold, the rain, and sometimes freezing rain, to pay respects to Coretta King for her long life of giving.

The press reported that many people from around the nation drove, flew, and caught buses to bid farewell. Many who stood in line for hours were finally unable to pay their respects because the Park Service was forced to close the doors to the historic Ebenezer Baptist Church. The line continued to form past the midnight hour. So many people came because Coretta continued her husband's work, loved people and was known to be a fair person.

During the week vigils and memorials were held throughout the country in remembrance of Coretta. On Monday February 6, Coretta's home church, Ebenezer Baptist Church, held two tributes to her. The afternoon musical tribute featured many artists, including Atlanta's own Gladys Knight, who performed "You Are the Best Thing That Ever Happened to Me." Roman Catholic archbishop Wilton D. Gregory, Ebenezer senior pastor Raphael Warnock, Oprah Winfrey, and Coretta's niece and author Alveda King Beal, all spoke of Coretta's giving spirit. The evening service consisted of tributes to Coretta's enduring faith, offered by Rev. Markel Hutchins, Rev. Kenneth Flowers, Rev. Al Sharpton, Rev. Amos Cleophus Brown, and Rev. Harold Alphonso Carter, Sr. Tributes from Coretta's loving friends were given by the Honorable Andrew Young, Mrs. Juanita Abernathy, Mrs. Xernona Clayton, and Ms. Dora McDonald. Tributes from her beloved community were given by Dr. Steven Lawry, president of Antioch University; Dr. Johnetta Cole; and Dr. Lawrence Carter, Sr. Tributes to Coretta's noble works were delivered by the Honorable John Lewis, Dr. Bernard LaFayette, Dr. C. T. Vivian, and Dr. Jesse Jackson. The

Coretta Scott King Memorial Choir, the famous Spelman College Glee Club, and the renowned Morehouse College Glee Club sang throughout the program.

On February 7, Coretta's six-hour Celebration of Life began. Ebenezer Baptist Church could not seat the estimated 10,000 people expected to attend, so services were held at New Birth Baptist Church, where Coretta's daughter, Bernice King, is an assistant pastor. Coretta Scott King's homegoing attracted many people from all walks of life—from dignitaries to janitors. In attendance were four United States presidents, President George W. Bush and Mrs. Bush, former President Bill Clinton and Senator Hillary Clinton, former President George Bush, and former President Jimmy Carter and Mrs. Carter. All four presidents spoke. Despite differences with Coretta, President George W. Bush stated, "I've come today to offer the sympathy of our entire nation at the passing of a woman who worked to make our nation whole. Her journey was long and only briefly with a hand to hold, but now she leans on everlasting arms. In all her years, Coretta Scott King proved that a person of conviction and strength could also be a beautiful soul."

Former President Bill Clinton challenged African Americans to keep the King Center for Social Change as our own instead of turning it over to the government to own and operate. He went on to say, of Coretta and Martin, "They understood that the difficulty of success does not relieve one of the obligation to try." Former President George Bush, Sr. stated, "Our world is a kinder and gentler place because of Coretta Scott King." Former President Jimmy Carter stated, "They [Coretta and Martin] overcame one of the greatest challenges of life, which is to be able to wage a fierce struggle for freedom and justice and to do it peacefully." President Carter continued, "The support of King and other Civil Rights figures in 1976 legitimized a Southern governor as an acceptable candidate for president."

Close family friend and Massachusetts Senator Edward Kennedy stated, "For decades, she was the wind at our back as we worked to uphold civil rights laws."

Coretta's close friends and Civil Rights pioneers also spoke of her. Former President of the Southern Christian Leadership Conference (SCLC), Joseph E. Lowery, read a personally written poem in eulogy of Mrs. King. He went on to say, "She extended Martin's message against poverty, racism and war." Atlanta mayor Shirley Franklin asked, "Who among us will join the freedom choir? Who among us will sing Coretta's song with courage and conviction, to smooth the cries of hatred, economic exploitation, poverty, and political disenfranchisement? For whom does the bell toll? It tolls for you and for me." Rev. Bernice King, daughter of Martin and Coretta, delivered her mother's eulogy. Rev. Robert Schuller, noted television preacher and founder of the Crystal Cathedral, gave the benediction.

Harry Belafonte, one of the King family's closest friends, had been invited to speak at the funeral but was conspicuously missing. No one was closer to the Kings than Harry Belafonte. He carried an insurance policy on Martin that helped Coretta take care of the children after Martin's assassination and provided the King family with a maid during the many years of the movement. He was a member of Dr. King's inner planning circle and was a major leader in the many very necessary SCLC fundraisers. It was therefore surprising that Belafonte was not present at the funeral. It was rumored and later appeared in the nation's press that President George W. Bush had said that if Belafonte, who has been critical of his administration, attended the service, he would not.

Coretta Scott King requested that she be buried next to her husband in the Reflection Pool at the King Center for Social Change. Following the funeral services, she was laid to rest in a temporary mausoleum across from Martin Luther King while a duplicate mausoleum is being built for her.

Who was this woman who won international renown as a voice for justice and a place among America's greats? How had she touched so many? How had she risen to national prominence and, after her husband's assassination, risen again to touch the soul of America and of people around the world?

We might begin her story fifty years ago, in Alabama, where the newly married Coretta lived with husband Martin and daughter Yolonda while he served Dexter Avenue Baptist Church.

CHAPTER 2

CORETTA

Coretta Scott King, also known as Mrs. Martin
Luther King, Jr., has been a symbol of the new image of African American womanhood since the days of the Montgomery
bus boycott, which had its beginning on December 1, 1955.

A bus carrying twenty-four African American people
seated behind twelve white people moved slowly through the
Court Square of Montgomery, Alabama. Although it was an
unusually warm day, there was a Christmassy atmosphere about
the square—the same square where, before the Civil War, slaves
had been auctioned.

Among the twenty-four African American people was an
attractive woman, Mrs. Rosa Parks, wearing rimless glasses. She
was tired from a hard day's work as a seamstress for the Fair
Department Store. She sat silently.

The bus pulled to a stop at the Empire Theater. Six white
people boarded. The bus driver, following the traditions of
Alabama and Southern segregation, asked the African American people to give their seats to those who had just boarded

the bus. Three persons moved immediately, but Rosa Parks remained in the first seat behind the section reserved for whites, while all other seats were filled. To yield her seat meant she must stand while a white man would take her seat. Rosa Parks did not move. The driver again asked Mrs. Parks to move, but she refused. The myth is that Rosa Parks had tired feet. She later said she did not remember telling anyone she had tired feet. Not really understanding all the reasons why herself, she just decided not to move.

A police officer was summoned, and Rosa Parks was arrested for violating the city's segregation laws.

Rosa had challenged the bus system many times, but she was never arrested until December 1, 1955.

Four years prior to this incident, a bus driver had physically removed Rosa Parks from a bus. Rosa had boarded and paid at the front of the bus and walked directly to the "Black Only" section. She had refused to get off the bus and re-enter through the back door.

African Americans were forced to pay their fare at the front of the bus, then walk outdoors, regardless of the weather, and re-enter through the back door. This was done under the laws of Southern segregation to prevent African Americans from walking too close to white people.

Rosa said she never followed that rule. She always walked directly to the "Black Only" section.

Many times a bus driver would drive off before an African American could walk back outside and re-enter through the back door, leaving him or her waiting for the next bus and having to pay an additional fare.

After that earlier incident, Rosa chose not to use the bus system; instead, she walked. However, she boarded the bus that day because she was pushed for time. She had to prepare dinner for her sick mother and her husband and later attend a meeting for youth of the National Association for the Advancement of Colored People (NAACP). When she boarded the bus, she had not noticed that this was the same bus driver who had physically removed her from the bus four years earlier.

Mrs. Parks, a person of great charm with an impeccable reputation and character, was one of the most respected persons in the community. There was something mystical about this shy, gentle lady going to jail. The effect on the African American community was profound.

Mrs. Parks's defying of local segregation laws and her arrest unified, for the first time, the whole community. The discontent of an entire African American community moved in one direction. For the first time after some three hundred years of slavery, a total community went all out to defend the honor of an African American woman. African American women had not known the real protection of males since their uprooting from Africa and placement in slavery. They were feeling what it meant to have a sense of male protection as community leaders joined together to do something about the treatment of Rosa Parks.

For years, African American males were intimidated in front of their women—usually while their women urged them to remain calm because they feared that the result for their men would be jail or harm. African American women now saw their men revealing a masculinity that previously had been suppressed.

Rosa Parks triggered a chain of events that started the greatest African American Civil Rights Movement in the United States, thereby also giving rise to the greatness of a twenty-six-year-old man, Martin Luther King, Jr. Her refusal to give up her seat came one year and two months after the Kings' arrival in Montgomery, Alabama, the first capital of the Confederacy.

King's new prominence gave rise to the first opportunity for African Americans to see an image of an African American woman, Coretta King, keep the home fires burning while her man went out to bring home justice.

The stories of United States history, the movie concepts, all show the man going out to make justice a reality for his wife, children, and country. African American women had seen their men go off to war and in some cases death, but they knew justice would not be possible for them in a society where nonequality existed for African Americans. The men who followed King's leadership in the years to come, facing police dogs, fire hoses, and possible death for justice, would give the children of African American women an image of new African American heroes.

Coretta was the first African American woman thrust into prominence by her husband. Franklin Delano Roosevelt had brought his wife, Eleanor, into the public eye, as John F. Kennedy later did for Jacqueline. At last an African American man, Martin Luther King, Jr., had done the same.

Prior to Coretta, it was emphasized to African American women that they had to make it on their own as insurance against poverty. The difficulty African American men have had in securing proper jobs created a situation in which African

American women have felt they must succeed alone. Even now, more African American women than African American men go to college. It is the reverse in the white race.

At that time the best example held up for African American girls of an African American woman making it on her own was Mrs. Mary McLeod Bethune, a daughter of slave parents, who founded an institute for girls in Daytona Beach, Florida, in 1904. This institute later merged with the Cookman Institute for men at Jacksonville, Florida, to form the Bethune-Cookman College at Daytona Beach. Mrs. Bethune was at the White House regularly. She served as an observer for the United States State Department at the founding conference of the United Nations in 1945. During World War II she assisted the secretary of war in selecting officer candidates for the Woman's Auxiliary Army Corps. Mrs. Bethune died in 1955. Her place in the sun as an African American woman had not been superseded until the new image of Mrs. King appeared.

In September 1954, the young Kings had begun their first pastorate at the Dexter Avenue Baptist Church. The congregation was composed largely of professionals and teachers at Alabama State College, a state-supported institution. When the boycott began, Coretta was adjusting to her role as a minister's wife and to her new role as a mother, having just given birth to her first child two weeks previously, on November 17, 1955.

E. D. Nixon, a Pullman porter, was one of the first persons to hear of Mrs. Parks's arrest. He had once served as president of the Montgomery branch of the NAACP, and Mrs. Parks had been his secretary. As soon as Nixon heard of her arrest, he went to post bond for her release. No one was more troubled by Mrs. Parks's arrest than Mr. Nixon.

Nixon called Martin the next morning and suggested that African Americans stop riding the buses as a protest against Rose Parks's arrest. Martin agreed.

That night a meeting of leaders and ministers was held at the Dexter Avenue Baptist Church. Ministers who were present agreed to speak to their congregations on Sunday. They left the meeting knowing the tremendous importance of getting people to refuse to ride the buses. They also left the meeting with a plan to have seven thousand leaflets printed and distributed, notifying the community of the bus boycott.

A maid who could neither read nor write asked her white employer to read her leaflet to her. The employer could hardly believe her eyes. She read:

> Don't ride the bus to work, to town, to school, or any place, Monday, December 5. If you work, take a cab, or share a ride, or walk. Come to a mass meeting Monday at 7:00 P.M. at the Holt Street Baptist Church for further instructions.

Outraged, the employer called the newspaper. By Saturday morning the planned boycott was on the front page. African American leaders were delighted. A white newspaper had given them wider coverage and notice than they had planned. The leaflet had been printed word for word.

On the eve of December 5, 1955, Coretta was busy tending to her daughter, Yolanda, fondly nicknamed Yoki by Martin. For some reason Yoki was unduly fretful and began to cry. Between Yoki's crying and the telephone ringing, it was after midnight when the Kings retired.

Coretta and Martin were up early and were fully dressed by 5:30 A.M. They lived five feet from the bus stop. The first bus was to pass at about six o'clock, and they impatiently waited to see the success or failure of the boycott. They had concluded the night before that if 60 percent of the people remained off of the buses, the boycott would be a success.

Martin was in the kitchen finishing his coffee when Coretta called him to the window to see the first bus go by. The South Jackson line that ran past their house was used by more African Americans than any other line. The first bus was usually packed with people on their way to work.

"Darling, it's empty!" Coretta exclaimed.

The next bus rolled by in fifteen minutes. It was empty. The third bus carried only two passengers, both white. By the end of the day, it was apparent that the bus boycott was almost 100 percent successful. Alabama State College students were seen walking or thumbing their way to campus. Hundreds of working people walked while some rode in cabs or private cars. Men were seen riding mules, and a few horse-drawn buggies were observed.

At 9:30 that morning, Rosa Parks was tried for violating the city's segregation ordinance. Attorney Fred Gray, a brilliant young African American, defended Mrs. Parks. Mr. Gray was later to become the chief counsel for the protest movement. Mrs. Parks was found guilty and fined ten dollars plus four dollars in court costs. Mrs. Parks appealed her case. Usually people were not charged with breaking a segregation ordinance. They had been charged with disorderly conduct or charges had been dismissed. Mrs. Parks's conviction was the first clear-cut instance of a conviction of breaking segregation laws, thus giving a case with which to test the validity of the segregation law itself.

After the trial, the ministers met to discuss some sort of organization to guide and direct the protest. A meeting was called for three o'clock to make plans for the evening mass meeting at the Holt Street Baptist Church. The group gathered and agreed on an organization. They elected officers. The Reverend L. Roy Bennett was chairing the meeting. Rufus Lewis nominated Martin for president of the group. The motion was seconded, and in a matter of a few minutes, Martin Luther King, Jr., had been unanimously elected.

White citizens of Montgomery were saying that Rosa Parks's refusing to give up her seat on the bus had been a plot of the NAACP, but the truth was that Rosa Parks's actions had been her own. However, a month prior to the boycott, NAACP members had approached Martin about running for president of their organization. Martin had not seen any reason he shouldn't run, but Coretta had urged him not to since he was attending meetings every day and every night. She suggested it would be too much. Martin followed Coretta's judgment and later recalling the incident said, "Coretta's opposition probably resulted in one of the luckiest decisions of my life. For when the bus protest movement broke out, I would hardly have been able to accept the presidency of the Montgomery Improvement Association without lending weight to the oft-made white contention that the whole thing was an NAACP conspiracy."

Coretta was relaxing before dinner from a long day of telephone calls when Martin arrived home for the first time since seven o'clock that morning. Martin, somewhat hesitantly, told Coretta of the new position he had been elected to. He was not too sure what her reaction would be. Coretta was surprised, but she saw the great responsibility and felt he had no other alternative but to accept it. "You know that whatever you do, you have my backing," she said.

King often said that Coretta's sense of optimism and balance was his constant support in the days that followed. As he put it, "She placed her faith on the side of opportunities and the challenge for Christian service." No one had to tell Coretta that she and Martin would have less time to spend together and that there would be danger to them and Yoki in his new position. Coretta seemed undisturbed by the threat of danger.

People who heard Dr. King say from the pulpit, "Sometimes I feel discouraged in Birmingham, sometimes I feel discouraged in Chicago . . ." realized and commented about the tremendous strength and understanding Coretta had to possess to reassure and support her husband when he was left alone with the heavy burdens that went along with his role as an African American leader.

At ten minutes to seven on December 5, Coretta said good-bye to Martin as he left for the Holt Street Baptist Church for the mass meeting. There was a traffic jam five blocks from the church, and cars were lined up on both sides of the street. Martin parked four blocks from the church and walked. The church had been filled with people since five o'clock. Three or four thousand people stood outside the church. They remained there to cheer throughout the evening as they listened over the loudspeaker system.

After describing Rosa Parks's arrest to the people, Martin went on to say, "But there comes a time when people get tired.

We are here this evening to say to those who have mistreated us so long that we are tired . . . tired of being segregated and humiliated, tired of being kicked about by the brutal feet of oppression."

Martin justified the boycott as both morally and legally right, pointing out that the glory of democracy is the right to protest for right. He said that some people were comparing the boycott to the White Citizens' Council and the Ku-Klux Klan, but that in this method of nonviolent protest there would be no lawlessness. No white person would be taken from his home by a hooded mob and brutally murdered. No one would be intimidated. Martin urged persuasion, not coercion. He urged people not to force people to stay off the bus but to say to others, "Let your conscience be your guide."

"Our actions must be guided by our deepest principles of our Christian faith," the people heard Martin preach. "Love must be our regulating ideal. Once again we hear the words of Jesus echoing across the centuries: 'Love your enemies, bless them that curse you, and pray for them that despitefully use you.'"

Mrs. Parks was introduced from the rostrum, and the people reacted by giving her a standing ovation. A new spirit was born. A new love was born. A new way was born.

The boycotters were asking for three things: courteous treatment from drivers; seating on a first-come, first-served basis; and employment of African American drivers on predominately African American routes. The bus company and city officials would not agree to these terms.

The city officials began a get-tough policy. Car pool drivers were stopped and asked to show their licenses and insurance policies. They were given tickets on any excuse. Riders waiting for someone to pick them up were threatened with arrest as hitchhikers. Most drivers stood firm, but some quit, fearing their licenses might be revoked or their insurance canceled. Some quit, feeling they could not remain nonviolent in the face of police abuse.

On the forty-seventh day of the boycott, Thursday afternoon, January 26, 1956, Martin was driving home from his church office with a friend, Robert Williams, and the church secretary, Mrs. Lilie Thomas. They picked up three people going their way. Martin was stopped by an officer and showed his license. Another officer across the street said, "That's that damn King fellow." Martin was allowed to go on, but two motorcycle policemen followed. One was still following them three blocks later. Robert Williams cautioned Martin to drive carefully and obey traffic regulations. Martin drove slowly and cautiously. As Martin stopped to let out the three passengers, the policeman arrested him for speeding thirty miles an hour in a twenty-five-mile-an-hour zone. Without question Martin got out of the car. He told Robert and Mrs. Thomas to notify Coretta.

Martin had not been in jail long before a jailer led him into a little room in the front of the jail. Martin was fingerprinted.

Martin's good friend, Ralph David Abernathy, was the first to arrive as the news spread of Dr. King's arrest. When he tried to get Martin out on bond, the officials told him he had to bring a certified statement from the court asserting he owned sufficient property to sign a bond. When Ralph noted that the court was closed, he was told he would have to wait until morning. Ralph asked if he could see Martin and was told no one could see him until ten o'clock the next morning. Known for his cool persistence, Ralph asked if it would be possible to pay a cash bond. The jailer reluctantly answered yes. Ralph dashed out to his church to call someone who could produce cash.

In the meantime, a crowd of African Americans began to gather outside of the jail. The number grew so large as people came from all directions that the jailer became alarmed. Rushing into the fingerprinting room, he told Martin he could go and ushered him out. Martin was released on his own bond. The jailer returned his possessions and said his trial would be at 8:30 A.M. Monday morning. He was driven home by a deacon of his church, where Coretta greeted him with a kiss of relief.

From that night on, Martin's commitment to the freedom struggle was stronger than ever. Coretta reassured him that she was behind him.

Telephone calls, all day and all night, plagued the Kings. Coretta took the brunt of the threatening and obscene calls, often while she and Yoki were home alone. Crudely written letters and cards came in the mail every day.

On January 30, four days after Martin's arrest, Coretta was sitting in the living room talking to Mrs. Roscoe Williams. They heard a sound Coretta first believed was a brick thrown on the porch, but her instinct told her to get to the rear of the house where two-and-a-half-month-old Yoki was sleeping. Halfway to the back, Coretta realized a bomb had exploded. It sounded to her as though the entire front of the house had been blown away. She could feel the cold air moving through the house. She thought to herself, "Well, it finally happened."

Her thoughts were on Yoki, who was still asleep, but for a moment she hesitated, not knowing what to do. She tried to think of someone to call. Then she and Mrs. Williams decided to go into the bedroom. At that moment the doorbell rang. Coretta froze in fear. During that terrible moment, she thought the person or persons responsible were coming in. She kept trying to decide what to do about the baby. At that instant a voice called out, "Is anybody hurt?" Coretta knew then she had friendly callers. She went to the living room and saw friends gathering in front of her home.

The telephone rang. A woman was on the other end saying, "Yes, I did it, and I'm just sorry I didn't kill all you bastards."

There had not been as much damage as Coretta had first feared. The bomb split a pillar on the porch and shattered the front windows. The living room was filled with broken glass and smoke.

The sound of the explosion had been heard many blocks away, so the word reached a mass meeting where Martin was speaking almost at once. Martin noticed people looking at him. People rushed in and out of the church. Ralph Abernathy looked worried. Martin was convinced that whatever was going on involved him in some way. He called Abernathy, S. S. Seay, and E. N. French over to him and asked what had happened. Abernathy told him gently but directly that his home had been bombed. Martin did not know until he reached home that Coretta and Yoki were safe. When he saw that his wife was composed and not bitter, Martin said he himself became calmer. Yoki slept through the entire ordeal.

The people outside the house were very angry. Martin went out and told them to put away their sticks and stones and weapons. He pointed out that this was a nonviolent struggle. The people went home.

The bombing caused Coretta to do a great deal of soul-searching. Her father came in the middle of the night to take her and Yoki home for safety, "until," as he put it, "everything blows over."

"I really wouldn't be happy if I did go," Coretta said. "I would rather stay here with Martin."

Mr. Scott feared that the opposition was armed, and he thought that Martin should move into the background and let someone else lead for a while.

Martin's father was there too, urging her to go, but Coretta refused. Daddy King argued it would be better to be a live dog than a dead lion, but Coretta told Martin's father that her place was with Martin.

That night Coretta lost her fear of dying. She committed herself more deeply to the freedom struggle, as Martin had done four days previously, when jailed for the first time in his life.

That night was particularly hard for Martin. Except for his sister Christine, his family and friends urged him to reconsider his position. He was visibly shaken by the close call his wife and child had had, but he and Coretta stood their ground. They both saw in a real way that they could and would be subjected to abuse and violence, but their belief that God was with them and their firm conviction that their cause was right, right enough to die for, left them determined.

Later Coretta said, "The first time I realized how much I meant to Martin in terms of supporting him in what he was doing was the morning after our home was bombed. At breakfast Martin said, 'Coretta, you have been a real soldier. You were the only one who stood with me.' I realized what I had done was to give Martin support at a time he needed it most."

Despite Coretta's decision, she went through a period of great uneasiness. Martin had times of frustration too. The thought that someone would destroy him and his wife and child put him to the test. It was with much misgiving that two weeks later he prepared to keep out-of-town speaking engagements he had committed himself to prior to the bombing.

It was decided that Coretta would go to Marion, Alabama, to visit her parents for a few days and then on to Atlanta to visit Martin's family. Martin was to join her in Atlanta for their return to Montgomery. During that week away from home, Coretta was surrounded by people who were extremely afraid. She grew very depressed. Anxiety built up within her.

Coretta came to grips with the overwhelming anxiety she felt. Later she said, "I could not continue to live that way. I rejected an impulse to figure out a way."

"I know we are right and we are going to have to stand up for what we believe," Coretta decided. She spent a great deal of time in prayer. She came to the point where she could pray, "Lord, help me to do not my will but thine."

The bus boycott had been going on for three months when, on February 21, a grand jury met and decided the boycott was illegal. One hundred boycotters and leaders were arrested. Martin was speaking in Nashville, Tennessee, when he learned there was a warrant out for his arrest. He rushed to Atlanta to pick up Coretta and Yoki. He wanted to get to Montgomery immediately to be with his friends.

Martin arrived in Atlanta. The time had come for Coretta to voice her resolve. Martin's family gathered in the kitchen. Mama King was very upset, and Daddy King was advising his son. A heated discussion over Martin's return to Montgomery developed. Fearing the noise would frighten Yoki, Coretta left the kitchen to take her child to another part of the house.

Martin interpreted Coretta's departure incorrectly. He told Coretta she had run out on him. Coretta explained her concern for the baby. Then she said, "I didn't run out on you. And I want you to know that the time comes in every man's life when there are decisions he has to make for himself and no one can make them for him. He may have to stand alone. But I want you to know that whatever you decide to do, I'll be with you."

Coretta and Martin returned to Montgomery. Martin gave himself up voluntarily.

On March 19 the trial was held. After four days the trial ended. Martin was found guilty of violating the state's antiboycott law. He was sentenced to pay a five-hundred-dollar fine or spend 386 days at hard labor in the county jail. An appeal was filed, and Martin and others were released on bond. Coretta and Martin left the courtroom smiling. They were cheered by a large crowd.

Two months later, on May 11, an appeal hearing was held in federal court. Three judges heard the case. It took the judges three weeks to reach a decision. The decision was that the segregation laws governing city buses in Montgomery were unconstitutional.

Lawyers for the city of Montgomery took the case to the United States Supreme Court. Montgomery lost again. On

November 13, 1956, the Supreme Court declared Alabama's bus segregation laws unconstitutional.

After 382 days of walking for freedom, fifty thousand people in Montgomery had won against injustice.

Of her Montgomery experience, Coretta said, "We were unable to predict success or failure. Faith was our guide and our future was a thing of conjecture. I am thankful that I am living in the second half of the twentieth century and that my life has been one of service and meaning. Not many people are fortunate enough to have something to which they can dedicate their lives."

Winning the struggle in Montgomery and the ability of Coretta and Martin to stick to a fight secured a new image for African Americans. Coretta's calmness under pressure and her strength forged for her an indelible place in the hearts of many people. She inspired her race magnificently.

CHAPTER 3

A CHILD OF STRUGGLE

Coretta Scott King was a highly versatile individual in her own right. As one of Mrs. King's admirers said, "Coretta King could not be an ordinary anything."

She was first an accomplished musician who studied voice with the Metropolitan Opera star, Mme Marie Sundelius. She often performed during their extensive travels in the United States, Canada, Mexico, Europe, India, and Africa, and visited dozens of countries.

While touring India with her husband in 1959, Coretta was invited to sing for many groups in cities, towns, and villages throughout India. When describing Coretta's warm, expressive, soprano voice, the music critic of the *Times* of India, a leading newspaper, wrote:

> Mrs. King rendered two Negro "spirituals" which stood out
> for their grace and beauty of expression. Her second song,
> "Nobody knows the trouble I've seen," had sweet and plaintive
> strains. . . . Mrs. King . . . invested her songs with a rare glow
> and intensity of feeling.

Coretta developed and performed the Freedom Concert for the Civil Rights Movement. The concert combined readings, music, and poetry and presented the history of the movement. The proceeds from the concerts went to the Southern Christian Leadership Conference. Once when Martin feared the SCLC could not meet its payroll, a check came in the mail and saved the day. The check was for the amount due Coretta for performing one of her concerts.

Mrs. King's life was filled with so much activity, with family, home, and Civil Rights involvement, that she curtailed her music career. She found an outlet for her love of music in the choir of the Ebenezer Baptist Church, where she could be found singing on Sunday mornings. It was not unusual to hear both Coretta and Christine, Martin's sister, featured as soloists for the morning. Or if you lived in the Atlanta area, you might receive an announcement by mail, inviting you to a recital presenting Christine. The invitation could have come from Coretta.

Coretta King was also a gifted speaker. She spoke with a quiet fervor of the movement. Her sincerity of purpose rang through her words. She had substituted for her husband occasionally but appeared in her own right before church, civic, and school groups throughout the nation.

Most people admired Coretta King for her steel will and composure, but some criticized her, saying that she was almost too cool or too calm. Looking logically at the role she played in her husband's life and in the Civil Rights Movement, what other type of person could have done as well? She had the love, strength, and determination needed. The question then becomes, What forms or produces a Coretta Scott King?

Coretta was a child of struggle. She worked hard for everything she got. Working hard was not difficult for Coretta, because her parents were beautiful examples of spunk and hard work.

Coretta's father, Obadiah Scott, born August 24, 1899, managed to get a sixth-grade education, which was considerable for that time due to the wide neglect of education for African Americans. Commenting about the success her father had later on in life, Coretta has said often, "I wonder how far he could have gone if he had had the opportunity of getting a high school education."

Obie Scott's family roots run deep in the soil of Alabama's Perry County. The family owned property there since the Civil War. Three generations of Scotts have lived on the family farm, located in a farm community about nine miles from Marion, Alabama, just outside of Alabama's Black Belt.

The freeing of slaves did not mean freedom for African Americans. They merely moved from toil with chains to toil without chains. They had become the servants of America. If white people wanted cotton picked or a house built, they went to an African American man. If a white woman wanted babies cared for, she went to an African American woman.

Some African Americans saw education as the way to move away from servanthood into the mainstream of American life. Some saw owning property as the way. Obie Scott cast his lot with the landowners.

Obie married a pleasant, attractive woman named Bernice McMurray. Bernice, born February 11, 1905, had only a fourth-grade education, but she had a talent and deep appreciation for music.

Obie Scott was intelligent and highly industrious and determined to do well by his family, which had grown to five by 1930 with the birth of a son, Obie Leonard, born April 22. The Scotts also had two daughters. The eldest girl, Edythe, was born December 13, 1924, and Coretta was born April 27, 1929.

Although the base for their future was ownership of land, the Scotts came to believe a good education was a must to secure the future of their children and to prepare them for competition in American society. Mrs. Scott told her girls they were going to college even if they had only one dress to wear, and so in 1948 and 1949, with the assistance of scholarships the Scotts' three children were all in college at the same time.

Obie Leonard, who later became a minister, attended Central State College in Wilberforce, Ohio, for two years. In 1966 he was one of the first African Americans to run for political office in the state of Alabama since Reconstruction days. He ran for the office of tax collector. He lost the race but was the leading contender in the primary.

Mr. Scott combined a trucking business with raising chickens. He was the first African American to own a truck in his community. For a while he worked beside white men hauling lumber. He was an excellent worker, and his employer rewarded him for jobs well done. The white men resented Obie very much.

During the Depression the Scott family, no matter how hard Obie worked, faced hard times. They barely eked out an existence. Obie's business sense, direction, and truck placed him in direct competition with white men, and as money and jobs grew scarcer, their resentment multiplied. Obie was stopped on highways and threatened with guns.

Obie Scott continued to press for work to take care of his family, all the while trying to reassure them. He repeatedly told his children, "If you look a white man in the eyes, he won't harm you." His theory was not necessarily logical to his children and caused them great concern. They were afraid he would one night go out and never return.

It could very well be that this early adjustment to the presence of danger prepared Coretta for the life of tension and threat of danger she was to later lead.

The only time Obie Scott was met with an actual physical attack was in 1947. By that time he was trucking, owned a grocery store, and was operating a taxi on Saturdays. It was the taxi service that brought about the attack.

Obie had applied for a license for his taxi, but it had not come. He had received permission from a deputy to operate his cab that day and had driven to Greensboro, Alabama, to a barber shop.

An off-duty policeman called Mr. Scott out of the shop to question him about the cab. As Obie Scott was attempting to explain the circumstances, the policeman grew very angry, lost his self-control, and struck Mr. Scott, knocking him unconscious.

To Obie Scott, a God-fearing, honest man who believed in following rules and regulations, the experience was humiliating and had a profound impact on his life. But being of strong will, Obie was able to put this experience behind him, as he had an incident that had happened seven years earlier when he began to operate a sawmill.

In spite of threats, Obie had invested his savings in a sawmill, only to have it mysteriously burned to the ground two weeks after it had opened. At the mill's burning, Mr. Scott suffered a great financial setback. The knowledge that an African American man's attempts to succeed were hampered because of the way others viewed his color had an unsettling effect on him. But showing his strong will and determination, Obie bought a truck and bounced back to grow more successful in his business efforts.

Speaking of her father, Coretta said, "In 1951 he built a modest home. On the family farm he raises corn, peas, potatoes, cotton, and other garden vegetables. He raises hogs and cows and has a chicken farm where he raises more than four thousand chickens at a time. My father can be considered a success by any American standard. He is a man who worked and built a successful life for himself, in his own home community, impoverished though it is."

The child Coretta has been described as being highly intelligent and very aggressive by nature. Her brother said, "She always tried to excel in everything she did. And she made good marks." A high school teacher reported Coretta was very intelligent and respectful of her elders.

Coretta herself admitted that she was a tomboy and had quite a temper. "My mother said I was the meanest girl. I used to fight all the time."

During a car ride in 1967 at the SCLC annual convention held in Atlanta, Mrs. Scott was asked what Coretta was like as a child. She began by agreeing with everyone else, "She was a very bright child." When asked about Coretta's reported temper, Mrs. Scott began to smile and took a moment to think.

Perhaps she was comparing her daughter then, a staunch advocate of nonviolence and peace, to the little girl who delighted in pelting her brother and playmates with sticks and stones and various other objects close at hand. By the time Mrs. Scott concluded her thoughts, she was laughing and shaking her head in the affirmative. "She was pretty mean all right."

At this moment Dr. King entered the car in which Mrs. Scott was seated. He said, "Mother," and gave Mrs. Scott a kiss on the cheek. The obvious affection between son-in-law and mother-in-law was a testimony to the warmth Mrs. Scott radiates.

When it came time for Coretta to enter school, she had her first real contact with racial prejudice, yet at that age she was hardly aware of the fact. Coretta joined the other children in walking four or five miles to the Crossroads School. As she grew older, she realized there was something unfair about white children in the neighborhood being driven to Marion schools in buses while African American children had to walk to Crossroads School.

Crossroads was a one-room frame building with a wood-burning stove. Two teachers taught all six grades. Coretta finished her first six years of education at Crossroads, the school that, Coretta says, "did not do much to prepare me." Nevertheless, whatever the school offered, Coretta received. She had been the top student in all her classes.

Coretta's next several years were spent at Lincoln High School in Marion, a semiprivate institution run by the American Missionary Association of New York. Lincoln was established during Reconstruction days. It functioned with white and African American teachers.

Coretta's tuition and board had to be paid at Lincoln. Like so many other African American teenagers, she had to leave home early Monday morning to get to high school and did not get back until the weekend because schools were not within walking distance, nor were buses provided to reach the African American high school many miles away.

Here is where the quiet determination of Mrs. Scott came into play. Growing tired of children being away from home, she, to the amazement of others, secured a bus. And as unusual as it was in those days for a woman to do, she drove the bus to and from school every day. The trip was ten miles each way, forty miles a day.

Coretta saw the school issue as a gross injustice. She committed herself to getting an education so she could use her education as an instrument to change the conditions she had grown up under. She was determined to help others coming behind her.

Lincoln High School opened new worlds of thought for a growing, inquisitive Coretta. It awakened in her a compelling drive "to be somebody" and to serve God. She sensed her service somehow would come through music.

Coretta, like her mother, sister, and brother, had a good voice. Her interest in developing her musical talent came to life at Lincoln. She played the trumpet and sang in the chorus, appearing as a soloist in recitals and musical productions. It was, in fact, Coretta's high school teacher who first inspired her to follow music as a career. Coretta began to study voice and piano with Miss Olive J. Williams.

Lincoln's choir toured several Northern cities during the time that Coretta's older sister, Edythe, was a member.

One concert had been at all-white Antioch College in Yellow Springs, Ohio. The concert had been so well received there that the Antioch administration sent scholarship applications to Lincoln.

In 1943 Edythe became the first full-time African American student to live on the Antioch campus. She was given a full scholarship for one year. Antioch had taken definite steps to integrate its student body. Finding that being a pioneer student was difficult, Edythe later transferred to Ohio State University, where African Americans were not a novelty. Edythe earned a master's degree in English from Columbia University in New York City and a master of fine arts degree in theatre arts from Boston University.

In 1945, upon completion of high school as valedictorian of her class, Coretta left for Antioch with a partial scholarship she had received from Antioch. Coretta considered her leaving for the North and Antioch an answer to her prayers. When Coretta attended Antioch, African Americans were no longer such a novelty, and yet they had not been completely accepted.

"I came North with a good deal of doubt about the wisdom of doing so and with a great deal of fear that I wouldn't be able to fit into the very different environment," Coretta wrote in an Antioch College magazine. She knew, however, that at a Northern school she would gain an advantage in helping the underprivileged as well as "the chance to better my condition and to acquire prestige to earn my living." Many colleges in the North were considered better than those in the South.

Most students at Antioch had attended better schools than Coretta, and their parents were professional people. Coretta realized she was competing with young people ahead of her educationally and culturally. Aware of her disadvantages, she appreciated the experience as a proving ground for her own abilities to meet life's challenging situations.

Coretta chose elementary education. She planned to be a teacher to serve the children of her race, but she included in her program many music courses.

Coretta gained a wide variety of job experiences under the Antioch Cooperative Work-Study Program. Under this plan, students alternated a period of work with a period of study. The most difficult job experience, Coretta recalls, was when she served as a junior group worker at the Friendly Inn Settlement House in Cleveland, Ohio. Coretta was the youngest person on the staff that year and worked with groups from nursery-school age to retired people. "I did a lot of growing up that year," Coretta says.

While attending Antioch, Coretta sang in the choir at the Second Baptist Church in Springfield, Ohio, serving as soloist. The choir director wanted to present Coretta in concert. Her college teacher encouraged her.

In 1948 Coretta performed her first concert. This concert debut set the stage for her decision to enter a school of music after graduating from Antioch. Concerts followed later in Pennsylvania and Alabama.

When it came time for Coretta to practice teach, she faced her first unpleasant experience at Antioch. No preparation had been made for her to practice teach in the Yellow Springs schools, which had no African American teachers then. The supervisor of practice teaching wanted Coretta to go to Xenia, Ohio, to an all-black school nine miles away, or complete both years of teaching at the Antioch Laboratory School.

Coretta had grown up in an area of the South where seven thousand white people dominated three times as many African American people. Her reading and memories of Lincoln had developed in her a desire to be treated as an equal. Humiliated and hurt, and possessing her mother's strength and her father's perseverance, Coretta decided to make an issue of the fact that she should be allowed to practice teach in public schools regardless of her race. She rejected her supervisor's suggestion.

Coretta carried her fight for justice through various channels to the top authorities on campus. "I did everything I could, but my classmates would not support me," Coretta explains. "If we protest, all our practice teaching facilities may be taken away and none of us will get our degrees," they argued. One friend gave Coretta moral support, but she would not speak up. Some students wouldn't discuss the subject with Coretta.

Finally, Coretta went to the president, who said to her, "Corrie, there is nothing we can do."

Disillusioned and depressed, Coretta fought back tears. Everyone was casual, and nothing changed. Coretta faced her first big crisis as an African American. She felt Antioch had failed her.

I am a Negro and I'm going to be a Negro the rest of my life, Coretta thought. *I just can't let this kind of thing get me down.*

Coretta accepted that she could not teach in the public schools but vowed she would never go to Xenia to teach in a segregated school. She felt she could have had that experience had she remained at home. She agreed to teach in the Antioch demonstration school, a choice she concluded was "the lesser of two evils"—the same basis her future husband was to use in attempting to solve some serious race problems.

Singing was Coretta's great love. The chairman of the Antioch department of music advised her to apply for admission to Boston's New England Conservatory of Music and to the Smith Noyes Foundation for a fellowship. Coretta applied before graduating from Antioch in June 1951. She was accepted at the Conservatory and planned to specialize in voice while getting a degree in music. Although she hoped to build a career on the concert stage, she wanted to be prepared to do something else if necessary.

After graduation Coretta spent several weeks at home waiting word from the Noyes Foundation. She wanted to go to the conservatory on her own without assistance from her parents, even though at this point they were able to help her. She felt she had been dependent on them long enough.

Hearing nothing, a determined young woman left for Boston. She made up her mind to work at whatever jobs she could get to pay her tuition. Before she left home, her father told her, "I wouldn't go there without any money. What are you going to do if you don't get a scholarship?" He had given Coretta her train fare and expense money. She assured him she would get a job.

Coretta had arranged for lodging in the home of a wealthy Beacon Hill dowager, a descendant of the Cabots, who let out rooms to talented students. She had been a contributor to the Interracial Scholarship Fund at Antioch. Coretta was to pay seven dollars a week for room and breakfast.

On the way to Boston, Coretta called the foundation. She learned they had sent a letter to her home in Alabama advising her she had won a $650 scholarship. She arrived in Boston happy.

The fellowship covered only tuition, so Coretta was faced with earning room and board. A combination of pride and desire to be independent kept Coretta from writing home for money. She paid her tuition and arranged to work for her room and board by cleaning the fifth floor on which she lived along with two other students. She was also to clean two stairways. The problem was dinner. For several days Coretta's dinner consisted of Graham crackers, peanut butter, and fruit.

It was not the first time Coretta had known hard times. During Depression days she had hired herself out to hoe cotton in Alabama. It was, however, the first time in her life that she had known hunger. She was in the unique position of living at one of the wealthiest addresses in America and starving.

Coretta missed dinner two consecutive nights. She was down to her last fifteen cents. A friend understanding her plight invited Coretta to her home. Her friend assured her that she had confidence in her future. She handed Coretta an envelope. Coretta opened the envelope on the subway. She found fifteen dollars. Tears flooded her eyes as she acknowledged, "People and life are good."

Later the Urban League secured work for Coretta as a file clerk in a mail-order firm. Her financial picture began to improve after the first year. She applied for and began receiving "out-of-state aid" from Alabama, which was provided African American students who were barred from white Alabama institutions. This state-aid system more often than not resulted in African American teachers being far better prepared than native white teachers, because African American students were forced to leave the state and attended some of the best universities in the country.

Coretta's youth well equipped her for the trials she faced and was to face in the future. She had the strength and character of her father, who forged ahead to success over enormous obstacles. She also had the quiet determination of her mother, along with a deep sense of commitment and loyalty.

No less important was Coretta's beauty, which lent obvious credence to the cry, "Black is beautiful." This cry was best put into words by Malcolm X but best demonstrated by Dr. King's movement. Once African Americans looked negatively upon themselves. But with the Civil Rights Movement, they observed African Americans walking for justice in the street with no weapons, believing that if white America could just see the problems, then their problems would be solved. African Americans were met with bombs, bullets, fire hoses, dogs— and African Americans saw that black is beautiful, if only by contrast.

Rev. Dr. Martin Luther King, Jr., and his wife, Coretta, are shown outside Circuit Court in Montogomery, Alabama, on March 22, 1956. Martin was found guilty of conspiring the Montgomery Bus Boycott that began Dec. 5, 1955. (AP Photo/Gene Herrick)

Martin was welcomed with a kiss by Coretta after leaving court in Montgomery, Alabama, March 22, 1956. Although King was found guilty of conspiracy to boycott city buses in a campaign to desegregate the bus system, a judge suspended his $500 fine pending appeal. (AP Photo/Gene Herrick)

Dr. Martin Luther King is given a welcome home kiss by his wife Coretta, upon his return to Atlanta following his release from Reidsville State Prison on bond, on October 27, 1960. Their children, Yolanda, then 5, and Martin Luther III, then 3, joined the welcome celebration. (AP Photo)

Coretta Scott King, 1963. © Bernie S. Faingold, Denver, Colorado. Faingoldphoto.com. All rights reserved.

Martin Luther King, Jr., 1963. © Bernie S. Faingold, Denver, Colorado. Faingoldphoto.com.

Martin and Coretta sit with three of their four children in their Atlanta home, on March 17, 1963. From left are: Martin Luther King III, 5, Dexter Scott, 2, and Yolanda Denise, 7. (AP Photo)

A moment of personal triumph: Martin and Coretta, along with his secretary, Dora McDonald, are greeted as they arrive in Oslo, where he was presented the 1964 Nobel Peace Prize during ceremonies on December 10. (AP Photo)

Martin and Coretta lead off the final lap to the state capitol at Montgomery, Alabama, on March 25, 1965. Thousands of civil rights marchers joined in the walk, which began in Selma, on March 21, demanding voter registration rights for blacks. Rev. D. F. Reese, of Selma, is at right. (AP Photo)

Martin was accompanied by Coretta as he arrived at the Atlanta airport, on October 30, 1967. He was en route to Birmingham, Alabama, to serve a five-day jail term for a conviction stemming from a 1963 civil rights protest. (AP Photo)

The Rev. Martin Luther King, Jr., speaking in Selma, Alabama, in February 1968. (AP Photo/Charles E. Kelly)

CHAPTER 4

MARRIAGE

Coretta, rather reserved and introspective as a very young woman, had many friends in Ohio but was somewhat isolated socially in Boston. A voice student from Atlanta, Georgia, Mary Powell, told Coretta about a young man from Atlanta who was attending Boston University. Mary had told the young man about Coretta, and he wanted very much to meet her. Dr. Benjamin Mays, president of Morehouse College, was a staunch supporter of the gentleman in question, argued Mary further. Mary mentioned the man's name—Martin Luther King, Jr.—but when she mentioned he was a minister, Coretta's interest dwindled. She was sure he was like all the other ministers she had known at home—conservative, pious, old, and narrow-minded. Mary insisted this was not true. Coretta finally told Mary she could give Martin her telephone number.

Martin telephoned one Thursday evening in February 1952. He talked about twenty minutes, taking time to mention subjects like Napoleon and Waterloo. A curious Coretta agreed to meet Martin on her lunch period the next day.

Martin arrived in a green Chevrolet, a gift from his parents. Coretta decided he was too short. The meeting went badly. Martin, determined, was hinting marriage on their very first date. Coretta remained silent, wondering about this unusual young minister. He was unlike any other minister she had ever known.

Coretta later said she had an "eerie feeling" when she met Martin. She often said, "While my husband was being prepared for the job he was to do, I feel that I was being prepared also to be his helpmate. When I think back over my life experience, I feel very strongly that it was meant to be this way."

Martin took Coretta to concerts, movies, driving, and dinner. The more Coretta saw of him, the more she liked him. "There was something about him that sort of grew on you," she said.

Coretta was impressed with Martin's driving sense of mission. His hope of contributing to his race and humanity was very strong. His feelings were similar to hers. Martin talked about his concern for underprivileged people. He was determined to fight to improve things. Martin's feelings caused Coretta some doubt. He had come from a middle-class background and had not known the conditions she had.

Martin pressed for marriage, at the same time urging Coretta to ask herself whether she could be the wife of a Southern minister. He asked her if she would fit in. He wanted to use his education to help African American people in the South, although life in the North would have been easier.

Coretta was in a dilemma. Did she love Martin enough to accept? Martin wanted a woman to come home to. Could she give up her dream of becoming a concert artist? She had envisioned herself traveling—beautiful gowns, curtain calls, tall suitors waiting at the door with roses. Friends told her Martin would never amount to much and that it would be blasphemous to sacrifice art for love.

Martin won. Martin and Coretta were married June 18, 1953, on the lawn of Coretta's Alabama home. Thus ended a courtship of sixteen months. Martin's father performed the ceremony.

The couple traveled back to Boston, where they completed their education. Together in purpose and aim, Martin did a few household chores while Coretta attended classes. The blending of lives had begun.

Coretta's life had been similar to Martin's in some respects. She came to books early, as had Martin. Like Martin she learned easily. So easily did Martin learn that he entered Morehouse College in Atlanta at the age of fifteen. At eighteen he was ordained a minister and elected assistant pastor of Ebenezer Baptist Church, where his father was pastor. His maternal grandfather had been pastor there before Martin's father.

Coretta had depended on scholarships a great deal. When Martin graduated from Morehouse in June 1948, he was offered a scholarship to Crozer Theological Seminary in Chester, Pennsylvania. Daddy King turned it down and paid Martin's way. He believed scholarships should go to the poor.

Martin had spent part of the time at home and part of the time on campus while attending Morehouse. At Crozer he gained a wonderful sense of adulthood and personal responsibility. He was six hundred miles from home. For the first time he was beginning to meet, know, and compete intellectually with white students, just as Coretta had done at Antioch.

Martin was one of six of his race on the Crozer campus. He felt about his personal growth as Coretta had hers at Antioch. She said, "I know now that I gained new understanding about my own personal worth, and that I no longer was haunted by a feeling of inadequacy . . . just because I was Negro. I enjoyed a new self-assurance that encouraged me in competition with all people, on their ground or mine."

Like Coretta, who had her first real disappointment when she could not practice teach in the public schools of Yellow Springs, Ohio, due to her race, Martin also met an incident of prejudice on the Crozer campus. Making friends had always been easy for him, but there was one student from North Carolina who seemed unwilling to accept African Americans. He often called them "darkies."

Martin did not know how deep this student's hatred went until during a prank several students disarranged the North Carolina student's room. The student himself had joined in similar pranks on other students, but when his own room was a shambles with his desk and chair overturned, he was furious. He immediately went to Martin and at gunpoint accused Martin of wrecking his room. Calmly Martin denied he had been in the group who wrecked the room. Other students persuaded him to put the gun away.

The matter was brought before both the student government board and the faculty. Martin refused to press charges. The student later publicly apologized. He and Martin eventually became friends.

At the age of twenty-two, Martin graduated from Crozer. He gave the valedictory address and earned the Crozer Fellowship Award of twelve hundred dollars for two more years of study, to earn a doctorate. Martin selected Boston University.

Coretta and Martin both came from families with three children. Each was the middle child. Each had an older sister and a younger brother. Both had fathers who dared to defy white people in the South, Obie Scott in business and the Reverend Martin Luther King, Sr., in leading many crusades for African American justice in Atlanta. He led the fight for equal salaries for teachers and won. He was instrumental in getting Jim Crow elevators eliminated in the courthouse. In all Daddy King's struggles against segregation, he was never physically attacked, a fact that had filled his children with wonder as they grew up.

Martin's maternal grandfather, A. D. Williams, was a pioneer leader of the Atlanta branch of the NAACP. He led an enraged African American group that forced Atlanta to build an African American high school by defeating a bond issue that made no provision for African American educational facilities. When the *Atlanta Georgian,* a Hearst paper, called the protesters "dirty and ignorant," Williams led a boycott of the paper. It was estimated that six thousand readers dropped the paper in a single day. The boycott led to the death of the *Georgian.*

In contrast to Coretta's rural life, which was better than that of other African American families in the community, Martin was raised in comfortable economic circumstances in the city. Although born in 1929, Martin was never touched by the Depression. Daddy King once said, "We've never lived in a rented house and never ridden too long in a car on which payments were due." Martin's mother, Alberta Williams King, was always impeccably dressed.

Time neared for Coretta and Martin to decide what they wanted to do upon completion of school. Martin had offers from two Northern churches, two Southern churches, and three different schools. They elected to accept the pastorate of the Dexter Avenue Baptist Church in Montgomery, Alabama. Their choice was in keeping with everything Martin wanted to do.

In September of 1954, Coretta and Martin moved to Montgomery. The period of time between September 1, 1954, and December 5, 1955, the first day of the bus boycott and the beginning of the vast Civil Rights Movement, found two extremely happy people in a big white frame parsonage at 309 South Jackson Street.

Throughout this time Martin continued to work on his thesis, having completed all other requirements for his degree before leaving Boston. He wrote several hours in the early morning and several hours each night. He completed his thesis in the spring and was awarded a Ph.D. in Systematic Theology on June 5, 1955.

No matter how busy Martin was, he had a knack for making Coretta feel needed and a working partner in all he did. She typed the first draft of his thesis, and he dedicated his first book to her.

After December 5, Coretta saw less of Martin, but she was actively involved, because as the movement developed, their home was used as an office and meeting place. Coretta accepted all the mail and sorted it, saving important items for records. She handled the phone calls and relayed information vitally important to a smooth-running operation.

As requests for him to speak out of town became more frequent, Martin left home without a worry because he felt that

Coretta's appearance at the bus boycott mass meetings that he was missing would give the people some sort of assurance.

Martin told the story of the Montgomery struggle in his first book, *Stride toward Freedom*. The reviews were excellent, and he started out on a tour of several Northern cities. He was fulfilling terms of the contract with his publishers and at the same time getting away momentarily from the tensions of the Southern struggle. To one who had had his home bombed and had received daily threats for preaching brotherhood and rights for all, a trip to the North seemed like temporary relief from pressure.

On September 20, 1958, King sat in the shoe department of Blumstein's Department Store in Harlem, New York City, autographing books. Martin was signing his name when forty-two-year-old Izola Ware Curry directed a question to him.

"Are you Martin Luther King?"

Martin answered affirmatively, scarcely looking up.

"I've been looking for you for five years," Mrs. Curry said and plunged a letter opener into his chest.

For Martin, a great champion of African American rights, to be the target of one of his own race astonished the nation. Izola Curry was later found to be mentally incompetent and was admitted to the Mattewan State Hospital for the criminally insane.

Stunned African Americans who believed in Martin paused to pray for his recovery. The fate of their leader and their new image hung in the balance. Praying and crying African Americans watched television screens as Coretta King, wearing a dark turban hat, her face revealing her concern, deplaned in New York. She was enroute to be with her husband at his bedside.

The letter opener was touching Martin's aorta. In fact, it had penetrated the outer layer. A sneeze or cough would have meant instant death. Coretta feared Martin might die before she could reach him.

Three hours of surgery were required to remove the letter opener. Martin remained on the critical list for several days. Coretta's calmness under pressure brought hope to the followers of Martin. She symbolized the strength of African American womanhood and all that is fine and noble.

Coretta spent her time between Martin's tenth-floor room and an office set up for her on the first floor by the hospital officials. From this office Coretta accepted calls and conducted the business of the Civil Rights Movement.

Even after Martin was well enough to travel to his home in Montgomery, Coretta handled the details to be sure Martin would not overwork. She flew to Washington, D.C., to take over a youth march for him. Harry Belafonte and Jackie Robinson led the march with Coretta. Coretta read Martin's speech for the occasion. Those close to the movement credit her with holding it together.

Coretta saw her role as a supportive one to Martin. She consistently stated, "I have taken my responsibility as a wife and mother seriously, as I take my role of wife to the leading symbol in the Civil Rights struggle. I have tried to understand and fulfill these roles. I am aware of my personal limitations. At every point I have believed that the case was most important, and I have been willing to make the necessary sacrifices."

Coretta admitted to the temptation to demand more of her husband's time and attention, but she realized that Martin belonged to the world. He was not free to be the same kind of husband and father as men not in public life.

Even when Martin was the busiest, Coretta said, "It pleases me greatly that Martin is admired. So I don't mind sharing him as he shakes hands and signs autographs for his many admirers." Her understanding was tremendous, because Martin had a minute for everyone no matter how important or unimportant they were. He was never known to be abrupt or rude to anyone.

Coretta always wanted the world to know what a great man her husband was. She spent a lot of time on the telephone attempting to explain to outsiders who criticized him what he was doing.

In many ways she was a very traditional housewife. In those precious moments of having Martin home alone, Coretta delighted in preparing his favorite dishes, especially home-made vegetable soup. She took great pains to see that their few moments together went unmarred by forgotten details. She made it a point to see that buttons were sewn on his shirts and that he had his special kind of shoes and that his wardrobe was intact.

Coretta was an excellent hostess, and no matter how busy she was, she was always able to go into the kitchen and prepare something when Martin came home with guests for dinner on short notice or even on no notice at all.

Harry Belafonte, realizing the enormous amount of work Coretta had to do, hired and paid for a maid for the King family. Very few people see Coretta as the wife who budgeted and lived within Martin's ten-thousand-dollar-a-year income from his copastorship with his father at Ebenezer Baptist Church.

His Nobel Peace Prize money was divided between the Southern Christian Leadership Conference and five other civil rights organizations, and what he earned from speaking and writing went into the SCLC to carry on its work for civil rights.

Very few people in the United States, outside of police and firefighter and Civil Rights families, have lived with the fact that when they kiss and part for the day they may never see each other again. Living with this truth makes a family closer and more attuned to one another. There is little time for common annoyances to crop up.

In November 1960, just three months before the birth of their third child, Dexter, Martin began serving an eight-day jail sentence for aiding Atlanta students in a sit-in protest. Martin and Coretta had discussed and accepted this arrest as nothing to worry about. It was more or less routine.

However, while in the Atlanta jail, Martin was awakened from his sleep at four in the morning by gruff voices and a flashlight shining in his eyes. Those rousing him were policemen. They used unnecessary force. Martin's legs were chained while a pistol was held on him. When he inquired where he was being taken, he was told to "shut up." He was placed in a car, and after a frightening ride, not knowing his destination or the purpose, he was relieved when the car stopped at the Reidsville State Penitentiary. He was to remain there for six months at hard labor.

Several months before, Martin had been arrested on a minor traffic charge. He had failed to get a Georgia driver's license and was driving on his Alabama license. Due to Martin's part in the Civil Rights struggle, it was obvious that the authorities planned to make things as rough for him as they could.

Martin had employed an attorney, paid a small fine, and considered the incident closed.

What Coretta and Martin did not know was that his attorney had entered a plea of guilty on Martin's record. In Georgia this meant that for any infraction of the law in the following six months, Martin could be required to serve six months at hard labor.

Martin's arrest in connection with lunch-counter demonstrations gave the neighboring county the technical right to have Martin transferred from Atlanta to their county. The neighboring county officials were alerted when the newspapers reported Martin chose to go to jail in Atlanta rather than pay a fine.

Coretta, who had been to visit Martin the day before, was very distressed. Her baby would be born while Martin was in prison. The Reidsville Penitentiary was four hours away, eight hours' traveling time round trip. Not sure whether and when she would be allowed to visit, she worried that he might be physically abused.

One of Martin's great pastimes while in jail was reading and writing. He had written most of his book of sermons, *Strength to Love*, while in jail. His famed *Letter from a Birmingham Jail* was written while he was confined. Coretta worried that he might not be permitted his reading and writing supplies.

When news began to circulate about Martin's transfer, telegrams began to pour into the office of William Hartsfield, mayor of Atlanta at that time. At the height of Coretta's concern, the telephone rang. "Just a moment, Mrs. King," a long-distance operator was saying, "Senator John F. Kennedy wants to talk with you."

Coretta was puzzled.

"How are you, Mrs. King?" a warm voice inquired.

"I'm doing nicely, thank you, Senator," answered a very surprised Coretta. It is not often an ordinary citizen gets a call from a United States senator and particularly when the citizen is a member of the African American race.

"I was just thinking about you," continued Senator Kennedy. "I understand you are expecting a child. This situation involving your husband must be very difficult for you."

Coretta admitted it was.

"Well," continued Kennedy, "I just wanted you to know that I am concerned and we are going to do everything we can to help."

The next day Martin was released.

When questioned about his call to Mrs. King, Senator Kennedy answered, "She is a friend of mine, and I was concerned about the situation."

Some people were saying that this call had political undertones and that Kennedy was out for the African American vote, which actually did play a major role in his election two weeks later to the office of President of the United States.

Coretta argued that Kennedy took a great chance in calling her. He had a lot to lose by calling. She clung to the idea that Kennedy was simply helping a fellow human being. She maintained Kennedy made her feel he was genuinely concerned about the welfare of her family.

In 1963, seventeen days after Bernice Albertine was born, Coretta had her second talk with John F. Kennedy. He was now president.

Martin had been in Birmingham leading integration demonstrations. He had flown to Atlanta and taken Coretta and their fourth and last-born child home from the hospital. As usual, Martin and Coretta discussed his anticipated arrest. Neither was upset. Usually Martin was permitted one call from jail, and he promised Coretta he would call her.

Martin was arrested on Good Friday. When Easter Sunday came there was still no call. The chief of police, Bull Connor, would not permit Martin to call.

Coretta was very distressed. She was confined to bed and could not find solace in church services. Missing her first Easter service in years did nothing to relieve her anxiety. Coretta was beginning to believe there was no hope in hearing from Martin. Near despair, Coretta called Wyatt T. Walker, Martin's executive assistant, who was in Birmingham.

Coretta asked Wyatt if she should make a statement to the press. She felt if the nation knew Martin was being held in isolation someone might come forward to help.

Wyatt listened sympathetically and said matter of factly, "I think you should call the president."

A little doubtful, Coretta asked, "Do you think he would talk to me?"

"He would have to talk to you," Wyatt responded.

Still hesitating, Coretta asked Wyatt to try to get a note through to Martin to see if Martin thought she should telephone the White House.

As the day ended, Wyatt called Coretta back. He had been unable to make contact with Martin. Wyatt this time spoke firmly and positively. "You have no other choice than to call President Kennedy."

Among African American people, news spread that King was being held incommunicado. Someone in Birmingham called

Chattanooga, Tennessee, saying Dr. King had been hanged. When the news was checked out, it was discovered that somewhere in Birmingham he had been hanged in effigy. Alarm was growing.

President Kennedy's father was very ill. Coretta knew the president was in Palm Beach, Florida. She had no idea how to reach him. She tried routing a person-to-person call through the White House. She was unsuccessful.

The local operator in Atlanta was unusually helpful and told Coretta she would try to get a number from Kennedy's Palm Beach headquarters. Fortunately, Pierre Salinger, President Kennedy's press secretary, answered the telephone. Coretta explained Martin's situation. Mr. Salinger promised to speak to the President promptly and have him call her back.

About forty-five minutes later, the president's brother Attorney General Robert F. Kennedy called, explaining that the president was with their father. To Coretta, Robert Kennedy seemed as warm as his brother had been two years earlier. The attorney general promised to call Birmingham immediately and find out how Martin was doing. He promised to let Coretta know.

Coretta felt relieved. A few hours later Robert Kennedy called again. He had been unable to arrange for Martin to call home, but he was safe.

Early the next evening someone called upstairs to Coretta that she had a long-distance call. Coretta answered the telephone to find a somewhat annoyed operator.

"Will you please get your child off the line. The president of the United States is calling."

After a little coaxing, Dexter, then two, relinquished his rights to the downstairs extension.

The president spoke in his usual friendly, brisk manner.

"Hello, Mrs. King. How are you? I understand you talked with my brother yesterday. I'm sorry I couldn't call you personally, but as you know, I was with our father." President Kennedy went on to state he had been in touch with Birmingham by telephone and had arranged for Martin to place a call soon.

President Kennedy informed Coretta that the FBI had been sent into Birmingham and had been in touch with her husband. He was fine.

President Kennedy appeared in no hurry to get off the telephone. He told Coretta to call either him, his brother, or Mr. Salinger if she had any other trouble. He asked about her health and was delighted to hear about the birth of their fourth child.

Martin said later that the behavior toward him had improved a great deal and suddenly. He did not know until Coretta told him that the change was because the president had intervened.

Martin and Coretta began to feel there was a genuine friend to African Americans in the White House. It was a great shock in November of that same year for Coretta to hear Martin's voice from upstairs calling to her that the president had been shot.

Coretta had known the president by telephone. She had not met him as Martin had, but her grief was profound. Staff members of the SCLC saw Martin more upset by the death of the president than they had ever seen him upset before. He went into seclusion for two days. While watching TV reports of Kennedy's death, Martin remarked, "That's the way I am going to go."

Throughout Martin and Coretta's marriage there were tensions and constant pressures due to the Civil Rights struggle. But rare moments of exhilaration offset all of the trials and tribulations suffered. One such moment was in 1964 when Martin was awarded the Nobel Peace Prize, and they attended the dinner that followed in Martin's hometown of Atlanta.

Coretta said at the time of Martin's honor, "I wish we could remain on this mountaintop forever. For the past ten years we have lived with the threat of death always present."

In retrospect, Coretta later said, "It was such a great moment, and I was so proud of Martin. Yet my feeling was one of joy and mixed panic because I realized that the honor carried with it great responsibility. I kept saying to myself, 'I don't know what the future will bring,' and it frightened me to think of it."

CHAPTER 5

MOTHER OF FOUR

Coretta's dream for her children began to take form in Alabama before Marty, Dexter, and Bernice were born, when Yoki was two and a half months old. The dream took form when a bomb was hurled on her porch, when Daddy King, Mama King, and Obie Scott pressed for their escape to the safety of Atlanta.

"I deeply believe," Coretta said, "I can only be worthy of seeing my dreams for my children come to pass by being willing to struggle, to sacrifice, even suffer, with an abiding faith in the future and unquestioning devotion to the principles of love, justice, and equality."

As Martin moved about the country, he told people about his children and his desires for them. Sometimes people cried when he told about Yoki and how she wanted to go to an amusement park in Atlanta. The park was called Funtown.

Yoki and Marty repeatedly watched a Funtown television commercial with a lively tune. Upon hearing the tune, Yoki and Marty would clap their hands and shout, "Funtown!" The commercial, very effective, stirred the children's interest.

Although many children were stirred, only some of them could participate.

Coretta and Martin knew that one day they would have to tell their children that Funtown was for white children only. When it was no longer possible to avoid it, Coretta and Martin explained to them that those who operated Funtown had decided to keep certain people out and those people happened to be "colored" people. Yoki began to cry.

"But I'm not colored," she protested.

As Coretta put it, "Intellectually of course Yoki knows that she is colored. Emotionally at that moment she wanted to reject anything about herself which seemed to make her unacceptable to others."

When Yoki stopped crying, she showed a reluctant acceptance with a "Well, I wish they had built a Funtown for colored."

Knowing how keenly hurt the children were about Funtown, Coretta pointed out to the children that Funtown represented the evils their father was fighting. Coretta took great pains to explain that the fact Yoki was not accepted did not mean that she was not as good or as sweet as any other eight-year-old child who did get to go to Funtown.

Coretta explained further that God made all people, red, yellow, white, black, and brown. God loved all his people. Coretta pointed out to Yoki that had God not loved all people of her race, he would not have made so many of them. Being the eldest of the King children and a very sensitive child, Yoki felt more sharply the impact of the daily pressures of being African American.

A white woman from California heard Martin tell the story of Yoki and Funtown. She wrote Yoki a note:

> Dear Yoki,
>
> I am a white American, the mother of three children, ages 8, 9, and 16. All of them, like you, cannot understand why some whites treat colored people so badly. But I know that when you grow up, lots more people will know that no matter if your hair is blonde, red, black, or dyed—inside we are all the same. Your Daddy and his friends are working to make this country better for everybody. You must be very proud of him.

The writer went on to invite Yoki and the King family to come to Disneyland in California.

In 1963 when Martin closed his "I Have a Dream" speech at the March on Washington, he voiced his dream that one day his children would be judged "not by the color of their skin but by the content of their character."

Each of the four King children was born or was very young during a crisis in the lives of the Kings. Yolanda Denise, born November 17, 1955, was two and a half months old when the King home was bombed in Montgomery, Alabama. Martin Luther King III, born October 23, 1957, was a year old when his father was stabbed in New York City. Coretta was pregnant with Dexter Scott, born January 30, 1961, when Martin was chained and carried to Reidsville Penitentiary. Fourteen days after Bernice Albertine was born, March 28, 1963, Martin was held incommunicado in a Birmingham cell.

"How can you rear normal children under great tension, always on the brink of danger and uncertainty?" was one of the questions most frequently asked of the Kings.

Coretta's answer: "We have faith in God, and we try to be good parents."

The year 1963 tested the security of the King children. That year much tragedy and heartbreak had occurred. There had been a series of church burnings in Georgia. A white postman, William L. Moore, who was convinced of the wrongness of racial discrimination and the customary treatment of African Americans, had chosen to walk from Tennessee, in the tradition of his work, to carry the message to the governor of Mississippi, Ross Barnett. Moore reached Alabama, where he was gunned down.

African American Freedom Fighter Medgar Evers had been slain in Mississippi. Six children had been killed in Birmingham, four in a church bombing and two following the bombing. One was killed by a policeman and one was killed by two white boys. In November the president of our country was assassinated.

The Kings felt their children were old enough and mature enough to have a sacrificial Christmas. Over the protests and arguments of friends, they explained to their children that Christmas was a time of sharing, and since so many people had suffered and lost dear ones, they wanted the children to share their Christmas with others and accept just one gift. Instead of getting a lot of things, they would make someone else happy. Martin and Coretta explained that they were not giving each other a gift.

The children not only responded, but Yoki and Marty bragged to their friends about their unusual Christmas. Dexter most likely did not understand, but he went along with his older brother and sister.

Dexter chose a fire truck, Marty and Yoki selected skates, and Bernice, "Bunny," was given a squeaky bunny rabbit. When Coretta viewed the happiness in her home that day she knew her children had understood. Martin gave the family almost the entire day, which he did on all holidays possible, leaving once to visit a friend who was in jail for attempting to desegregate a church.

Many people saw Martin as only a civil rights leader and did not have a picture of him as a family man. The King children loved roughing it up with their father. They would greet him with much shouting when he appeared. Martin had been the athletic type in school and enjoyed playing ball and swimming. His brother A.D. recalled Martin never being very passive on the ballfield.

One favorite roughhouse game of the King children always took place in the kitchen. It started when Yoki was very small, and it was loved by each child in turn. Martin would put the small child on top of the refrigerator, and the child would jump down into his father's arms. When they were older, the children jumped off the steps into his arms.

"I died a thousand deaths each time they played that game," Coretta says. In spite of her fears, no one was ever hurt.

New Year's Day of 1964, Martin, Yoki, Marty, and Dexter turned the living room into a handball court. When Coretta, fearing furniture breakage, protested, Martin assumed the air of an injured little boy and replied, "Where else do we have to play?"

Coretta, a mother under stress and tension, had one very hard task. It was hers to answer the children's difficult questions.

"Why can't Daddy stay home like other daddies?" Coretta would explain that their father was "one of God's helpers." As a helper he had to travel many places and help many people. This idea was not hard for her children to understand and accept.

"Why does Daddy have to go to jail?" was the most difficult question for Coretta to answer. It was difficult because the children had been taught that bad people are put in jail. Coretta had to explain so the children would not lose respect for their father and so they would get an understanding of what he did.

Coretta explained that Martin's being in jail was to help people also. She pointed out that some people did not have food, clothing, and nice houses to live in. Their father was trying to make these things possible for all people. The important thing was that the children know their father was in jail for doing good rather than doing bad.

Yoki and Marty were four and two when they first learned their father had been to jail. Yoki had come home from school crying because someone had told her that her father had been jailed in Atlanta. Marty began to cry too.

Coretta's gentle way of explaining helped Yoki and Marty not only to accept the notion of their father's helping others but to take great pride in that fact. Fortunately, they were young enough not to understand the hardships placed on an African American man in a Southern jail.

As Marty and Yoki grew older, Coretta explained more fully. She told them their father had been imprisoned for helping students in local sit-in demonstrations. Later that year lunch counters were integrated. Coretta took this opportunity to give assurance to her children.

"You see," she said, "I told you why Daddy went to jail." She explained that he wanted to make it possible for people to be able to go to places where they had not previously been accepted.

Later when Yoki learned from a television newscast that her father had been jailed in Albany, Georgia, she began to cry. Coretta thought perhaps the idea that Martin was confined so far from home made it a difficult time for Yoki. It was three-year-old Marty who saved the day.

"Don't cry, Yoki," Marty said. "Daddy's gone to help more people. He's already helped some people. But he has to help some more now. When he finishes, he'll be back." Marty did the perfect job of consoling his older sister. Like his father, Marty was deeply attuned to the feelings and moods of those around him.

Yoki at one point startled her mother by saying, "White people are prettier than colored people."

"Oh, no, that isn't true," Coretta said emphatically. "There are pretty people and others not so attractive in all groups."

"No, Mommy," Yoki insisted. "White people are just pretty and colored people are ugly."

Coretta got a few copies of *Ebony*, a leading black magazine. She could not and did not intend to let Yoki have a doubt about her value as a person *and* as an African American person.

Yoki and her mother looked through the magazines and saw many good-looking African American models.

"Isn't she pretty?" Coretta would ask. "Isn't he handsome?"

"Uh-hum!" Yoki exclaimed enthusiastically.

When Coretta's selling job had been accomplished, Yoki looked up at her mother. She was deeply impressed.

"Colored people are prettier than white people."

Coretta had to start all over again.

The death of President Kennedy was a traumatic experience for Yoki. She learned of the news before reaching home from school. Coretta held her child in her arms and tried to comfort her.

"President Kennedy is dead," Yoki said. "They killed President Kennedy, and he didn't do anything to anybody. Not one thing. Oh, Mommy! We aren't ever going to get our freedom now."

Coretta explained to Yoki that the president's death was very upsetting to both her and her father. She tried to reassure Yoki that God was over all and they would still get their freedom.

A few days after Kennedy's death, the King family was seated at the dinner table. Marty directed a question to his father.

"Wasn't President Kennedy your friend, Daddy?"

Before Martin could reply, Marty concluded, "Yes, Daddy, he was your friend. He was your best friend."

To Coretta, Marty's remark was the perfect personal epitaph from the King family to a president and person they loved so much.

As Yoki watched a television show dealing with nonviolence and race, Yoki predicted, "They're going to kill all the Negro leaders, and then the rest of the Negroes will agree to segregation." Coretta realized that Kennedy's assassination had focused Yoki's attention on the fact that her father could be killed too.

Several days after Kennedy's death, Yoki said to her mother, "Every time I think about it, I get a pain in my stomach."

Coretta later stated she could only hope that her children would not ever consider the white man "the enemy" because of the acts of some white men. "As hard as we have tried to make sure that our children will not develop antiwhite prejudices, I must confess it is not an easy job in a world and in a city where they daily meet reminders that they are being rejected because of their color."

The King children were well acquainted with events about them. During the Cuban Missile Crisis, Yoki said, "If they keep on talking about Cuba, I'm not going to live to be seventeen years old. I don't want to be blown up!"

Coretta reassured her eldest child quickly. She reminded Yoki that just the preceding year she had been one of fifty women, members of Women's Strike for Peace, who had gone to Geneva to talk to the heads of nations. The women were seeking to persuade the leaders to resolve their differences without war.

"You'll live to be seventeen, Yoki, even older," Coretta said.

Yoki thought briefly, shaking her head negatively. "Well, Mommy, I'll tell you one thing, you'd better be glad you lived to get grown!"

This was one of the rare times Coretta was at a loss to answer Yoki.

Coretta was asked many times what she wanted for her children. Invariably she answered, "I want my children to be free of prejudice against others and at the same time maintain a pride in and identify with their race.

"I want them never to become stifled, never to give in to situations calculated to make them feel they are less than or not equal to others. I want them to have quality, a sense of, as Martin had termed it, 'somebodiness.' I dream of my children becoming adults and raising their children in a world full of creative compassion and universal concern."

CHAPTER 6

ABIDING FAITH

The great motivating force in Coretta Scott King's life was her deep religious faith. It was a faith fed constantly by the unlikely happening. Coretta believed that God works through people. She said, for example, about the intervention of Senator Kennedy when Martin was taken in chains to the Reidsville Penitentiary, "Here is one more evidence of God's working, one of several of which have occurred in my life. There have been moments when my religious faith has been severely tested, when I have almost despaired. Somehow in the midst of these trying moments of darkness, a hope, a ray of light has always come to brighten my way. With a strong conviction that the cause to which we have dedicated our lives is right, I can go on with the faith that right will win and truth and goodness will ultimately triumph."

"When I think back over my own background and experiences," Coretta said, "I felt very strongly that it was meant to be this way." She feels her life of service and meaning was not sought, but "fell upon her."

Coretta's faith typified the nonviolent Civil Rights Movement of the South. She was not the only one involved early in the movement who believed that his or her life was directed in the channel that it took. Many Civil Rights workers have the feeling that they were in the right place at the right time, an answer to the anguished prayers of slaves and African Americans in the years of America's oppression.

It is natural that ministers played an active role as leaders in the struggle of the South, and so it was natural that the movement had religious overtones. The African American minister often was the only person free enough to lead the way in the Civil Rights struggle. His salary came from the African American community. A teacher, a maid, or any other worker could have been fired.

Southern ministers would have been and were leaders with or without Martin Luther King, Jr. But Martin had a rare gift. He was a leader's leader and a wise man. He saw each person's attributes and shortcomings and got the most out of each one's ability. He held together a group of activists who likely would not have been together without him.

Choosing the wrong person to lead African Americans in the South could have led to the mass murder of many African Americans, such as the killing of thirty-five African Americans by whites in Vicksburg, Mississippi, December 7, 1874, by those who would use force and gun-power to keep African Americans "in their place."

In Martin's wisdom and from his knowledge of his fellow activists, he selected a man who could articulate the religious mood of the movement and not conflict too much with the personalities of the other men, Ralph David Abernathy, to take over after him. Abernathy was a man who did not push himself ahead but committed himself to putting Martin forward as the leader. He was not a publicity seeker, and he was very loyal. A man of great humor, Abernathy went ahead of Martin when there was trouble and smoothed things out so Martin would not have to deal with the smaller problems when he arrived.

In the years of the struggle, events that have shocked most Americans or caused them to wonder have served to feed the faith of the religious who went into the streets to protest discrimination and to destroy the myth that African Americans were satisfied with the status quo.

In 1961, when CORE's first Freedom Ride buses rolled into Jackson, Mississippi, every person aboard those buses was committed to dying so others might be free. "No greater love has any man than that he lay down his life for his brother," says John's Gospel, and it bespoke the dedication of the Freedom Riders.

In Anniston, Alabama, whites had destroyed a bus and beaten the riders. One white professor from Detroit was permanently paralyzed by the beating he took. A white person participating would be more brutally attacked than an African American by Southern whites. They seemed more infuriated at the sight of a white man protesting for an African American man. If not beaten outside of jail, a white man would be severely beaten inside the jail by the white prisoners in segregated cells. An African American protester would be placed among the African American inmates, who knew they were all in it together, regardless of the circumstances.

Mississippi was judged the worst possible state in its treatment of African Americans. The killing of an "uppity nigger" occurred more readily there than in any other state. When the rivers were dragged for the bodies of three Civil Rights workers killed in Mississippi, the bodies of several other African Americans, the victims of murder, were found.

Because of the violence that the riders had already met and the reputation of Mississippi, there was little doubt in anyone's mind that the Freedom Riders would be killed. At home, wives prepared themselves and their children.

When word reached everyone that the riders had been arrested and no one hurt, their survival was considered a miracle in itself. Faith was fed once again.

The Freedom Rides broke down discrimination in interstate commerce, although some Civil Rights workers were quick to point out that these rights—the right to travel freely, to eat and to use restrooms and motels—were given because buses are involved in interstate commerce and not as an acknowledgment of African Americans being human beings.

Early in 1961 a bomb was hurled at the home of attorney Alexander Z. Looby in Nashville, where a boycott was under way. The blast destroyed the house and broke windows on the Fisk University campus and in Meharry Medical School. A story in a local paper stated that had the bomb not missed, had it gone inside the house rather than fallen short, landing against the foundation, the whole block could have been leveled. A casual reader who did not know that block would not know that it would have meant the destruction of Fisk University, of Meharry Medical School, housed in Hubbard Hospital, which was filled with patients and staff, and of dormitories, apartment buildings, boardinghouses, and homes.

A direct hit would have been a catastrophe that America could not have lived down. Mr. and Mrs. Looby escaped injury. The miss was indeed a testimony to some person's meaning an act for evil but God's meaning it for good. African Americans in Nashville had a feeling that this was a time "to be thankful for one's enemies, for it helps one to see how good God is to them."

The bombing led to a march of five thousand people on the mayor's office. That march and confrontation led to the pricking of the white conscience, thus ending the boycott and opening all eating establishments in Nashville to everyone.

One of the most unusual events that fed the faith of many happened in Birmingham, after the bombing of the Six-teenth Street Baptist Church, in which four girls in a Sunday school class were killed.

A march was being led by the Reverend Charles Billups. In every march the people had been met by policemen backed up by firemen with hoses. The hoses were said to have enough power to rip the bark off a tree. Well-dressed marchers straight from Sunday church services followed Billups. The group found their way blocked by the usual police and hoses commanded by Police Chief Bull Connor, who called out, "Halt in the name of the law."

"Move on in the name of the Lord," said Billups.

"Halt in the name of the law," commanded the police.

Billups dropped to his knees in prayer. The marchers fol-lowed suit. When Billups finished praying, marchers were cry-ing, firemen were crying, and policemen were crying. Billups stood up and said, "Move on in the name of the Lord."

"Turn on the hoses," came the order. The firemen looked at the police and then at the people.

"Turn on the hoses," came the order again.

Firemen dropped their hoses and walked away. The people walked on with Billups in the name of the Lord.

Those watching the news on television that day heard the newsmen saying, "For some unknown reason the marchers were not drenched by the hoses today," but to those whose faith was strengthened by the incident, God had stood by them once again. Later on when the strange happening was discussed, Billups could not remember what or how he had prayed, nor could the people.

Billups, a rare individual who had been struggling for African American's rights before Martin Luther King came into prominence, was killed in November 1968 by an unknown assailant in a yet-unsolved murder in Chicago.

Coretta's answer to people who wonder how she lived under pressure and fear was, "I do not live under fear. I do not think about it. In periods of tension you think more about the possibility of danger, but you go on and it becomes a way of life."

Coretta expressed joy at having been in Montgomery from the beginning. "I feel," she said, "this is a great time to be alive, and I'm thankful that God has seen fit to make me an active partner in this great emergence."

In the beginning of the protest movement, members of the Dexter Avenue Church volunteered to take turns spending the night at the Kings' home. Someone bought a gun and gave it to Martin. It stayed in the house about a week, and then Martin got rid of it.

A friend, Bob Williams, a professor at Alabama State College, slept at the Kings' home for a while after their house was bombed. He slept with his shotgun beside his bed. Every time a car stopped, Bob jumped. Martin finally said there would be no guns in his home. Nor would he let anyone guard him.

However, in 1964 Coretta began to feel strongly that Martin should have someone travel with him, "if only as a witness should something happen to him."

Martin agreed. Coretta felt this way for several reasons. During a convention in Birmingham, a white man slapped Martin. A short time later Martin was speaking at the Sunday Evening Club in Chicago, on a program that was to be televised. Just seconds before the program started, Martin spied the man who had slapped him seated with five other white men in the front row. There was no one Martin could tell to alert the policemen who were there to keep order.

Martin made his speech and nothing happened. Fortunately, when the program was over, police encircled Martin. The man who had slapped Martin was approaching him. Martin called to the man, who realized he had been recognized. He retreated.

Returning home from Selma, Alabama, one evening, Martin was recognized by a white man on the plane.

"What are you doing, King, reading about yourself?" the man taunted.

"No," replied Martin, "I'm reading about the president's tax bill."

The man stood up and began to curse. A steward helped the man into his seat. When he got to his feet once again, the steward grabbed him and pushed him back into his seat, where he remained.

Coincidentally, Bernard Lee was with Martin on that trip, and after that Bernard always traveled with him. On planes Bernard sat near the aisle and Martin by the window.

Coretta's faith was sorely tested many times. She was momentarily afraid when her husband was stabbed in New York. Her first thought was that the wound would be fatal. She sat on the side of her bed and prayed, "Lord, if this is the way for him to go, help me accept it." Coretta had her cry in the quiet of her room with God. No one saw her shed a tear after that moment.

The assassination of President Kennedy tried Coretta's faith too. She felt utter despair. Kennedy, the man who had helped her keep faith, was dead. It seemed to her at the time worse than seeing a member of her family die.

When Coretta saw Martin receive the Nobel Peace Prize, she recalled, "Somehow I saw in that experience a purpose, as though everything was taking place according to a plan. Somehow I began to believe that each experience is built upon a preceding one. This experience had special significance for me. It helped me and it strengthened me.

"You see, I had begun to be frightened over our involvement. But when I realized that these events were taking place as a result of the movement, I knew that they were not just isolated events on the stage of history and realized that there was a plan and purpose.

"I felt God was at work using people and situations to fulfill his purpose in creating a better world."

"So many people have asked me how I felt about things happening to Martin," Coretta wrote in an article in the *New Lady Magazine* in 1966, a black publication in California. "I thought I could anticipate and face them as realistically as possible without having the actual confrontation of the experiences. I thought about it as something I have to live with from day to day. It is ever present. I began to feel concern and began reacting. I became weak and depressed. I asked myself what was wrong with me, and I knew I could not live that way. I have to see my way clear. I have to find some kind of answer. I finally concluded that you experience periods of development and then you reach a plateau beyond which you do not go for a while. I had to renew my courage, my strength, and my faith to go the additional distance. I had to prepare for the days ahead because I did not know what they would bring. In about a week I began to feel better again. Right now I do not know, but I believe God is working. We are coworkers with God, trying to bring about the kingdom of brotherly love and peace. If he sees fit to use us, we must accept his will, knowing that all things work together for good for those who love the Lord. From this belief, I gain consolation and the faith to continue.

"I believe very strongly that a person must dedicate himself to what he believes. When you decide to give yourself to a great cause, you must arrive at the point where no sacrifice is too great. This is the first demand that is made of us in our great struggle for civil rights. I shall stand with Martin Luther King, Jr., my husband, as he faces them."

CHAPTER 7

MEMPHIS

In 1956 Martin Luther King's nonviolent protest methods brought African Americans the freedom to ride unrestrictedly the buses in Montgomery, Alabama. The movement mushroomed. In January 1957, the Southern Christian Leadership Conference was founded in Atlanta, Georgia, by ministers from ten Southern states. Martin was elected president.

Martin predicted then that people all over the country would think him a miracle man. True to his prediction, in the years to come, Martin Luther King was called upon to help free African Americans from various racial situations.

The African American garbage workers in Memphis, Tennessee, in March 1968, under the leadership of the Reverend James Lawson, striking for more pay and better general working conditions, were no exception.

Jim Lawson, a longtime friend of King's, better than anyone else had articulated the meaning of nonviolence as an approach in the Southern Civil Rights Movement. Jim had traveled in India and was a believer in Gandhi's passive resistance protest. He was instrumental in developing the nonviolent theory in the Nashville sit-ins in 1961, a protest so beautifully organized and representative of the people and the nonviolent theory that Martin had said Nashville had "the best nonviolent movement in the South."

The Nashville movement developed leaders who are still involved in the nonviolent struggle. Others besides Jim Lawson are the Reverend James Bevel, an organizer for people's movements, who possesses tremendous insight and was once one of the top brains and organizers in the movement; Marion Berry, former mayor of Washington, D.C.; Bernard Lafayette, who directs international workshops on Kingian nonviolence; John Lewis, United States congressman; and the Reverend C. T. Vivian, who directs workshops, gives speeches and sermons on race, racism, and contemporary American politics.

Martin King wanted to show his support for the nonviolent protest of the garbage collectors in Memphis, but at the same time he did not want to get bogged down there, for his main concern was his Poor People's Campaign, which was to climax in a march on Washington in April. This campaign was to unite for the first time all the nation's poor, poor whites from Appalachia, Puerto Ricans, Hispanic Americans, Indians, and African Americans. It was Martin's plan to go into Memphis, lead a march on March 28, 1968, and leave.

During the march, some young African American teenagers seized the opportunity to dramatize that although all African Americans believe in freedom, they do not all believe in nonviolence. They joined the ranks of the nonviolent protestors and then broke ranks and began throwing rocks and breaking windows. Martin, taken by surprise, tried to bring order but was unable to do so. His coworkers feared the outbreak of destruction would be used as an excuse for a racist to shoot Martin. King was steered away by a group of ministers and driven away from the scene.

This ruining of the peaceful march depressed Martin greatly. A sixteen-year-old boy was killed by a policeman during the disturbance, sixty-two people were injured, and some two hundred were jailed.

To some people it appeared King had led a violent march. To some it appeared he ran from the scene, deserting his followers. To some it seemed he had lost control of his people. To some it was an opportunity to say King should be denied the right to lead a march into Washington. The capital would be destroyed, they said.

Martin's plan to lead one march and leave Memphis had to be abandoned. He must lead another march. "Nonviolence," he told friends, "is on trial in Memphis." He could not concede the hour to violence.

On April 3 Martin said good-bye to his family in Atlanta and left for Memphis.

Martin sat for some time waiting for the departure of the flight. Once aboard the plane, he heard the voice of the pilot explain the delay. "We have Dr. Martin Luther King on the plane." The pilot went on to say there had been a bomb scare and the plane had been held on the ground until a complete baggage inspection had been made. According to the pilot, the plane had been kept under guard to be sure nothing would go wrong.

Because of the March 28 incident, Martin sent four staff members, Jesse Jackson, Hosea Williams, James Bevel, and James Orange, into Memphis to talk with the young people who opposed his nonviolent stance. He was to lead several rallies himself before Monday, April 8, the date set for the attempt at a peaceful march in Memphis.

The first rally was to be the evening of the day Martin arrived, and soon after registering into room 306 at the black-owned Lorraine Motel, Martin conferred with his staff. That evening at the Mason Street Temple the rally was a rousing success. The militants and the believers in nonviolence were together at the meeting.

Martin spoke, mentioning the plane incident. He told of threats in Memphis too, saying, "But it really doesn't matter with me now. Because I've been to the mountain top. . . . And I've looked over, and I've seen the promised land.

"I may not get there with you, but I want you to know tonight that we as a people will get to the promised land. So I'm happy tonight. I'm not worried about anything. I'm not fearing any man. Mine eyes have seen the glory of the coming of the Lord."

The people rose in unison. The applause was tremendous, a sign that unity for nonviolence could win in Memphis. Martin was hopeful.

The next morning Martin arose in a mood, it seemed to those near to him that day, of extreme cheerfulness and great jubilance. He spent most of the day with his aides in his thirteen-dollar-a-day room. He spent a great deal of the time discussing the importance of nonviolence with the staff. He showed great concern that white America had not responded enough to the nonviolent protests that had been conducted over the past decade.

Hosea Williams, speaking later of Martin's stressing nonviolence that day, said, "Dr. King really preached us a sermon.

He said the only hope of redeeming the soul of this nation was through the power of nonviolence. He talked about the life of Jesus and Gandhi and he told us, 'I have conquered the fear of death.'"

That afternoon Ralph Abernathy entered room 306 to find Martin eating a double order of fried catfish, a favorite dish of Martin's.

"Where's mine?" Abernathy asked.

"I didn't order one for you, Doc, but you may have some of mine," Martin said. (Doc or Doctor was a name those close to the Civil Rights Movement called each other as they went about during the racial ills of our nation.) Martin and Abernathy sat and ate from the same plate.

Early that evening Mrs. Samuel Kyles was preparing dinner at home. She and her husband were looking forward to having the evening meal with Martin, A.D. King, and several staff members and coworkers. Martin was looking forward to a good home-cooked meal. He often grew tired of restaurant eating.

While dressing for dinner, Martin conversed with Chauncey Eskridge of Chicago, former legal advisers of the SCLC.

"Chauncey," Martin said, "will you go tell Jesse to get ready?" As Eskridge left, Martin added, "And tell him to put on a tie." Chauncey left to find Jesse.

The Jesse referred to was Jesse Jackson, the twenty-six-year-old national director of Operation Breadbasket, a project of the SCLC. Jesse, a strapping former ballplayer, had turned down an opportunity to play professional baseball with the Chicago White Sox. He entered the University of Chicago's divinity school, leaving later to join the SCLC staff. Jesse seldom wore the conventional white shirt and tie. Rather, he leaned toward turtleneck shirts or the dashiki, African-type shirt.

"Tell Dr. King I'm comin'," Jesse replied to Chauncey, "but tell him I ain't goin' to put on a tie." Born in Greenville, South Carolina, well-educated Jesse spoke with a "down home" accent, leaving off *g*s at the end of words.

A short time later, Jesse, accompanied by Ben Branch, leader and saxophone player of the Chicago branch Operation Breadbasket band, started out to join Martin.

In room 306 at the motel, Martin finished shaving, a task he really never liked. He had very tender and sensitive skin. The next to shave was Abernathy. As Martin and Abernathy started to leave the room, Abernathy said, "I forgot to apply my after-shave lotion," and returned to the bathroom.

Martin stepped momentarily onto the balcony and looked down on the parking lot. As he did, he looked down on the parking lot and saw Jesse, tieless and wearing a green turtle-neck shirt.

Dr. King broke into a smile. "Jesse," he called, "I see you disobeyed me and didn't put on a tie."

"Dr. King," Jesse said as he looked up into the amused face of Martin, "I'm not goin' to put on a tie. I don't need to put on a tie to run with you all. A string around my neck has no relationship to my eatin'."

Dr. King was laughing. It had been a good day. He had accomplished a great deal with the staff. Plans for the forth-coming march were going well. And too, Martin's brother A.D. had been passing through the city on his way home to Lou-isville, Kentucky. He had stopped by the Lorraine and had an accidental meeting with Martin. The two had had a long, relaxed chat, something time had not afforded the King brothers often in recent years.

Jesse, looking up to the balcony again, asked, "Oh, Dr. King, you remember Ben Branch?"

"Oh, yes," Martin answered. King had remarked to others how he had enjoyed the moving rendition of one of his favorite spirituals, "Precious Lord," as done by the Breadbasket band during his last trip to a Chicago Breadbasket meeting. "I want you to play 'Precious Lord' for me tonight . . . and play it real pretty for me." King was referring to the evening rally during which the band was to play.

Ben's band combined jazz with spirituals, and their music reached four to five thousand people each week at the Saturday morning Breadbasket meeting on Chicago's South Side. Ben smiled and agreed to play Dr. King's request.

Solomon Jones, King's driver, looked up from beside the car where he was waiting for Dr. King. "Dr. King, you had better get a coat. There is a bit of a chill in the air."

Dr. King, who was leaning over the balcony, nodded in agreement to Solomon's suggestion. He appeared to be ready to move. Jesse, realizing that at dinner he might not have an opportunity to speak to Dr. King and desiring to have a few moments of Dr. King's time later to discuss programming, intended to ask for an appointment and said, "Oh, Dr. King."

Dr. King turned slightly in Jesse's direction and, starting to answer, said, "Yes?"

At that moment the sound of a gun blast rang out. Dr. King said only, "Oh," and lay on his back, having been wounded in the neck.

Abernathy had left the bathroom and was halfway across the room when the shot rang out. He was the first to reach King.

As others arrived they saw Abernathy's look of disbelief and heard his anguished voice saying helplessly, "Martin, Martin."

James Laue, a white Justice Department community relations man, dashed from his own room down the hall and applied a towel to the wound. Abernathy ran for another and larger towel when the first was blood-soaked. The Reverend Andrew Young felt for a pulse. Down in the parking lot where perhaps fifteen black people stood shocked and crying, James Bevel was on his knees in prayer. Abernathy kneeled down over his friend and began to pray softly. The Reverend Sammy Kyles, who had been in room 306 at the time of the shooting, covered Martin with a blanket.

CHAPTER 8

ATLANTA

The telephone rang in a lovely but modest brick house, the home of Martin Luther King, on the southwest side of Atlanta. The house was on the fringe of Atlanta's slum area and yet not far from the educational and cultural center of the African American community.

In spite of its location, the house contained some tokens like no other houses in the area. The most prized were a camel saddle from Egypt, a small ivory carving of Gandhi, and a painting entitled "Integration," done by the great-great-granddaughter of John Brown, an abolitionist who was hanged in 1859 during the Harper's Ferry raid.

It was not by accident that the King home had this particular location. Dr. King preferred to stay within the African American ghetto near the people he was serving. His previous house had not been in as good condition. The old house would not have been livable had it not been for Daddy King, who kept up the repairs for Coretta while Martin was away. They moved from it only when urban renewal was scheduled to come to the area.

The Kings had relocated before the actual date of demolition, and during the period of waiting for the destruction of the old house, SCLC used it as their Freedom House. It gave Coretta a good feeling to know that their old house was being put to good purpose.

Not only was living in the ghetto Dr. King's choice, but it gave more safety to his wife and children. Living close to friends who looked out for his family's safety was some assurance to King as he traveled. The opportunities for bombing and burning his home were lessened.

Coretta King, the person to be most affected personally by the shooting in Memphis, reached for the telephone.

Jesse Jackson had had the presence of mind to call Coretta before news of Dr. King could reach her coldly by way of radio or television.

After a momentary greeting, Coretta heard Jackson say, "Dr. King has been shot."

"Is he dead?"

"I don't know how bad it is, but I suggest you get a plane out right away," came Jesse Jackson's reply.

Soon the entire United States and the world would hear of the shooting. The news traveled rapidly by telephone, television, radio, and word of mouth.

The mayor of Atlanta, Ivan Allen, long considered a liberal and a man who had the respect of the African American community, was one of the first to rush aid to Coretta. Allen made Coretta's plane reservation, escorted her to the airport, and waited with her for the flight to Memphis.

Racing to the airport in an attempt to join Mrs. King was her close friend Miss Dora McDonald, personal secretary to Dr. King. Dora was the person who had run interference for Dr. King. She handled his affairs well and kept him free from small details. When he was most pressured, Dora even kept the staff from disturbing her boss.

On the car radio, Dora heard Dr. King had died. She drove faster now, anxious to reach Coretta before she could leave for Memphis.

The major news sources reported erroneously that Mayor Allen had informed Mrs. King of her husband's death. What actually happened was that Dora reached Coretta and Mayor Allen before they knew. Desiring to break the news to Coretta in some sort of privacy, Dora asked Coretta to accompany her to the restroom.

Dora later said, "I had only to take Coretta's hand. Coretta looked into my eyes and she knew."

Dora recalled that tears welled in Coretta's eyes. "A tear trickled down Coretta's face, but she never lost composure."

Mayor Allen went to confirm the report that Dora had heard on the radio. He came back to tell Coretta and Dora it was true.

Jesse later confided to close friends he was certain Dr. King had died instantly. "He suffered no pain, and he was happy to the end." Jesse added, "He was happy and laughing when he died. I didn't want to blurt out what I thought to Coretta. She needed time to get herself together."

As the ambulance had arrived at the scene of the shooting, James Bevel, seeing Martin placed aboard the ambulance, said, "I believe he's gone," voicing the same thought as Jesse.

Coretta had lived for more than a decade with the knowledge that death or harm could come to herself, her children, or her husband because of the role they played in seeking an end to racial discrimination against African Americans and injustices against the poor of all races. She was more prepared than most women to accept a personal loss such as hers and in the manner that it came to her. The difficulty was in realizing that the moment of acceptance had come.

Now a widow, her face frozen in grief, Coretta reentered Mayor Allen's car for the ride back home to her children.

Coretta attends the funeral of her husband at the Ebenezer Baptist Church in Atlanta, Ga., April 9, 1968. (AP Photo)

Coretta speaks during a news conference, April 6, 1968, about her husband's work and prospects for its continuance. Beside Mrs. King was Rev. Ralph Abernathy. (AP Photo/Charles E. Knoblock)

In the early days after Martin's funeral, Coretta is seen at her home in Atlanta, May 28, 1968. (AP Photo)

Coretta preached from the pulpit of St. Paul's Cathedral in London, March 16, 1969, the first woman ever invited to do so at a regular service in London's biggest Anglican church. (AP Photo)

Coretta shakes hands with Sen. George McGovern at a news conference in Los Angeles, where she endorsed his bid for the Democratic presidential nomination on May 18, 1972. Applauding at right is the church pastor, the Rev. Tom Kilgore. (AP Photo)

Top: Coretta Scott King is flanked by her son Martin Luther King III, right, and Rev. Joseph Lowery, president of the SCLC as she sings the civil rights hymn "We Shall Overcome" following a rally on the steps of the Lincoln Memorial in Washington, D.C., on August 27, 1983. (AP Photo/Ira Schwarz)

Bottom: Coretta, center, is arrested along with her daughter, Bernice, left, and son Martin Luther King III, outside the South African Embassy in Washington, D.C., Wednesday, June 26, 1985. The three were protesting the political policies of the South African government. (AP Photo/Charles Tasnadi)

Winnie Mandela gives a black power salute as Coretta Scott King speaks to the media during her visit at Mandela's home in Soweto, South Africa, Thursday, Sept. 11, 1986. (AP Photo/ Greg English)

Coretta is shown at a press conference in Atlanta, Jan. 11, 1986, to launch a ten-day celebration for the first national holiday for Dr. King. A poster depicting King is in the background. (AP Photo/Ric Feld)

CHAPTER 9

COURAGE

The day after Martin's death, Americans sat before their television screens watching Coretta King, hatless and dressed very simply in black, leave from the Atlanta airport enroute to Memphis to claim the body of her husband.

The plane on which Coretta and a group of friends were leaving had been chartered for her by Senator Robert F. Kennedy, who himself was murdered two months later. Kennedy was speaking in Indianapolis, campaigning for the Democratic nomination for president, when he learned of Dr. King's death. Kennedy immediately announced the death to the people who had gathered to hear him. The audience was predominantly African American. Kennedy then called Mrs. King to see what he could do, and the chartering of the plane was an outgrowth of that call.

The heavy downpour of rain fit the feeling of the day. Only newsmen and Mrs. Benita Bennett were on hand to see the group off. Among those accompanying Coretta on the flight were Dora McDonald, Jean Young (Mrs. Andrew Young), Juanita Abernathy (Mrs. Ralph Abernathy), the Reverend Fred

Bennett, and William Rutherford, both on the SCLC staff, and Christine Farris and her husband, Isaac.

In Memphis Abernathy had remained close to Martin. Having been the first to reach Martin, he told of his friend's eyes turning to him and of his attempting to speak, but he could not.

"He seemed to be trying to communicate to me with his eyes," Abernathy said, "His eyes seemed to be saying, 'Ralph, I told you this would happen, and now it's happened. But for God's sake, Ralph, don't let me down.'"

Ralph stayed with Martin through the ambulance ride to Saint Joseph Hospital. When Martin Luther King was pronounced dead at 7:10 P.M., Abernathy, against the wishes of co-workers, insisted on going through the awesome ordeal of the autopsy. Abernathy selected the casket that was to be used temporarily in Memphis and closed the top of the casket after an early morning memorial service. And he closed the hearse door as the casket left for the Memphis airport, where Coretta would be waiting.

When the top of the casket was closed, the men who had worked with King and who had taken the fastest possible transportation to Memphis when they heard of the shooting, broke down together. It was a policy that civil rights workers went to aid the other when he was in trouble. This time, lost in the hopelessness of the moment, they drew strength from one another by just being together. Coworkers and staff joined a two-mile-long procession of cars to the airport.

The casket was hoisted aboard the plane. Coretta stood in the doorway, a symbol of the African American woman who loses her mate to death if he dares to stand up for African

American rights, and on the ground watching Coretta and the casket, the men understood the profound suffering of an African American woman. The door closed. Coretta wept softly on the shoulder of a friend.

There had not been room enough for everyone to get aboard Coretta's flight. Abernathy and A.D. King had traveled with Burke Marshall, former assistant attorney general, and Earl Graves, former aide to Senator Robert Kennedy.

At the Atlanta airport, by 10:30 A.M. people had begun to gather in anticipation of Coretta's return. By that time the rain had turned to a mist. The crowd, a mixture of whites and African Americans, grew to three hundred. The crowd consisted of ministers, politicians, Student Nonviolent Coordinating Committee representatives, and people from all walks of life.

At 12:45 P.M. Mayor Allen, his vice mayor Samuel Massel, the Reverend Sam Williams, chairman of the Community Relations Commission, Mrs. Ann Moses, executive secretary to Allen, and Police Captain Morris Redding arrived together.

In one of the limousines the King children sat waiting. When the flight arrived at 1:30 P.M., the King children, Mayor Allen, and the Reverend Sam Williams were admitted aboard the plane.

A ramp was rolled to the rear of the plane. King's casket was lowered down into the waiting hearse. Coretta and her children stood watching the plane door. At the sight of them, the crowd began to sob. Coretta noticed the anguished crowd. "They are the ones who need help now; it's not real to me yet," she said.

The general public saw only the brave Coretta carrying on. Even in grief, knowing what to do and say to give courage to the believers, poor, African Americans, whites, and the depressed, was a gift of Coretta King.

When Coretta was seated in the car, the crowds pushed forward as if in need, just to touch the car in which she was riding. She gave a sad smile to the people. A procession of fifty cars started back to Atlanta. Scores of African Americans watched from yards, windows, porches, streets, and rooftops.

Mayor Allen was in the procession. He had explained earlier to newsmen that his purpose in being there was two-fold. He wanted to extend his sympathy to the King family on behalf of the city, and he wanted to be sure that Atlanta would not erupt in violence. Many people, including "militants," would be coming to town, and Mayor Allen wanted to maintain law and order. He left shortly after the procession arrived at the Hanley Bell Street Funeral Home.

A crowd had gathered at the funeral home. A few friends went inside with the King family. A weary, sleepless, and fasting Abernathy spoke softly to the people. He had not eaten since his friend's death. His last meal had been the fish Martin had shared with him. Abernathy had been to jail with Martin seventeen times, and each time they had fasted and prayed together the first twenty-four hours in jail.

"We are deeply honored by your presence and concern," Abernathy said, "for this is a dark day in the history of black people all over the world. We have brought our leader home." Abernathy then asked the mourners to give the King family a moment with the slain leader.

Realizing the funeral would be an enormous procedure, Coretta had called Wyatt T. Walker, Martin's former executive assistant, and asked him to take over the responsibility of planning the funeral. Only a short time before, Martin Luther King had installed Wyatt as pastor of the New Canaan Baptist Church in Harlem, New York. Wyatt arrived in Atlanta in a matter of hours.

Coretta, with the help of family friend Harry Belafonte and his wife, Julie, went about the task of selecting a permanent casket. Coretta had the body redressed. A teenage member of Ebenezer remarked later, "You know, Rev. King wouldn't wear any other kind of shoes than he had on in that casket. I was so happy when I looked down and saw what he had on his feet." The Belafontes remained at Mrs. King's side during the trying days after Martin's death.

On April 6, millions again watching their television screens saw Coretta emerge from her home to go to a press conference at Ebenezer Baptist Church, where Martin had served eight years as copastor with his father.

During that press conference, Coretta made her first public statement since Martin's death. She was appealing to distraught, angry African Americans who had seen their leaders die violently one by one: Medgar Evers had been killed in 1965 in Jackson, Mississippi; Malcolm X, who spoke eloquently to the poor and impoverished of the slums and ghettos, had been gunned down also in 1963. Now Martin Luther King, the greatest African American leader, had been gunned down.

James Meredith, first African American male to integrate the University of Mississippi, had been shot but not killed. He had been taken to the same hospital and operating room where Martin Luther King had been pronounced dead.

"Genocide!" was the cry. The story is told about two young boys seated on a bench on Chicago's West Side. The boys concluded, "If they will kill someone as good as Dr. King, someone as nonviolent as he is, then what chance do we have?" In utter angry frustration they went out and broke windows. They felt as so many African Americans did, that "survival is the name of the game."

There were those who did not follow King, had not followed King, but saw the opportunity to say to the white man, "Time is running out. Either I will have something, or you won't either." Some dramatized this feeling by taking home possessions from stores. The amazing thing is not that some wavered in this moment of violence against a great leader, but that their frustrations were directed toward property and not people. With very rare exception, those killed in what is termed *rioting* were African Americans. They were killed by police or National Guardsmen. The youth killed in the Memphis outbreak had surrendered to the police, according to some fifteen eyewitnesses.

It had been the feeling of the movement leaders that the death of King would lead to widespread violence. Many of them were amazed that so few people became violent, a testimony to a job well done by a disciple of nonviolence.

Nevertheless, a great deal of damage was done to property throughout the country. Forty-three deaths were recorded. The hardest hit city in the nation was Washington, D.C. It suffered three days of pillaging and burning. Ten of the forty-three deaths were in Washington.

A great deal of news space was given to pointing out the militancy of Stokely Carmichael, leader of the Student Nonviolent Coordinating Committee (SNCC), and comparing him with Martin, but no space was given to the fact that Stokely started out as a follower of Dr. King. He had tried the non-violent approach but thought the movement had not gained success fast enough. Stokely and others like him had seen the ruling for integrated schools, but substantial integration had not occurred. A voting-rights bill had been passed, but few registrars had been used to enforce the law. They began to say that a person should get free by any means necessary. Even at this point they still hoped that freedom could be for African Americans in America.

Stokely had marched with Dr. King as a good-looking curly-headed youth with hope in nonviolence. Stokely, now considered militant, and others like him, had given their word to Dr. King that they would cooperate with the nonviolent approach for the planned upcoming Poor People's Campaign.

Knowing one of her husband's great concerns had been that in the event of his death violence should not take over, Coretta was holding the press conference.

"My husband," came the low tones of Coretta's voice, "told the children that if a man had nothing that was worth dying for, then he was not fit to live. He also said that it's not how long you live but how well you live. My husband's work transcends his death. We knew that at any moment his physical life could be cut short, and we faced this possibility squarely and honestly.

"My husband faced the possibility of death with no bitterness or hatred. He knew that this was a sick society, totally infested with racism and violence, that questioned his integrity, maligned his motives, and distorted his views, which would ultimately lead to his death, and he struggled with every ounce of his energy to save that society from itself.

"He never hated, he never despaired of well-doing, and he encouraged us to do likewise. And so he prepared us constantly for tragedy.

"I am surprised and pleased at the success of his teaching, for our children calmly say, 'Daddy is not dead. He may be physically dead, but his spirit will never die.'

"Ours has been a religious home, and this, too, has made this burden easier to bear. Our concern now is that his work does not die. He gave his life for the poor of the world, the garbage workers of Memphis and the peasant workers of Vietnam. Nothing hurt him more than that man could attempt no way to solve problems except through violence. He gave his life in search of a more excellent way, a more effective way, a creative rather than destructive way.

"The response from so many friends around the world has been comforting to us, and many friends joined to make this tragedy bearable.

"We intend to go on in search of that way, and I hope that you who loved and admired him would join us in fulfilling his dream.

"The day that the Negro people and others in bondage are truly free, on the day hate is abolished, on the day war is no more . . . on that day I know my husband will rest in a long-deserved peace."

There were two things that Martin King had stressed he wanted in case of his death: his people to remain nonviolent and his friend Ralph Abernathy to move into his position. Coretta said at the press conference that Dr. King would be happy to know his closest friend had taken his place.

Martin had gone to Memphis to prove he could lead a
peaceful march because his last march had ended with violence. It was later discovered that some marchers had been paid
by Memphis police to incite window-breaking and violence.
It deeply troubled Martin to have his march disturbed. On
April 8, Coretta determined Martin would have the nonviolent march he went to Memphis to have and had scheduled for
that day, the day prior to the funeral, it turned out, and so she
boarded a plane chartered for her by Belafonte and close family
members and flew to Memphis.

Three other chartered planes accompanied Coretta from
Atlanta, loaded with people from all over the country. Some
of them believed Coretta should lead this march and some
believed she should not but were going to show support. Some
people on the chartered planes had never been in a march
before. They went because of Coretta. They felt Martin Luther
King had paid the supreme price for all African American men;
Coretta had paid a price for all African American women; her
children had paid a precious price for all African American
children.

Going into Memphis, the marchers were not sure what
the attitude would be among the young African Americans
of Memphis. When Coretta led a march that saw no type of
trouble, some believed that her brave appearance calmed those
who might have caused trouble. Memphis people joined in the
march. The crowd swelled to an estimated fifteen thousand
people.

The true strength and courage of Coretta emerged when
she rose to address the crowd. For her to lead a march had

surprised them, but to give a speech? Where did she get her strength? Respect flowed through the crowd. "That's quite a woman," men said. Tears rolled down the cheeks of men and women. The people seemed to draw strength from her.

"I want you to know," she began, "that in spite of the times he had to be away from his family, his children knew he loved them, and the time that he spent with them was well spent. And I always said that it's not the quantity that is important but the quality of time.

"My husband was a loving man, a man who was completely devoted to nonviolence. And he, I think, somehow was able to instill much of this into his family. We want to carry on the best we can in the tradition in which we feel he would want us to carry on.

"This hour to me means much more than just a time to talk and eulogize my husband. We loved him dearly, the children loved him dearly. He was a good father and he was a good husband. And we know his spirit will never die."

Coretta, looking toward the crowd, went on, "And those of you who believed in what Martin Luther King, Jr., stood for, I would challenge you today to see that his spirit never dies and that we will go forward from this experience, which to me represents the crucifixion, on toward the resurrection and the redemptive spirit.

"We must carry on because this is the way he would have wanted it to have been. We are not going to get bogged down, I hope, and from this moment on we are going to go forward. We are going to continue his work to make all people truly free and to make every person feel that he is a human being. His campaign for the poor must go on.

"He often said unearned suffering is redemptive, and if you give your life to a cause which you believe is right and just and it is . . . if your life comes to an end as a result of this, then your life could not have been lived in a more redemptive way. And I think this is what my husband has done."

The King children, Yoki, Marty, and Dexter, seemed to possess some of the same strength their mother had. They marched the long two miles and sat on the platform with her during the long program that followed the march. Bunny had to remain home because of a cold.

Belafonte had introduced Coretta. He described the bravery with which Coretta and her children had faced their new life as a fatherless and husbandless household. He described Coretta as a "beautiful black woman."

The crowd saw Coretta embrace and congratulate Ralph Abernathy, who gave his first major address since becoming the new president of SCLC.

To Abernathy and his wife, Juanita, fell the most difficult task of all. Following a Dr. King is a terribly difficult task. Abernathy's work was cut out for him. It wouldn't be easy for those who had followed King to quickly transfer their loyalty from him, to whom they had been emotionally tied and whom they trusted for guidance, to anyone else. Abernathy had worked in the background. Although he had gone to jail often and his home had been bombed, he was relatively unknown, particularly out of the South and in white communities.

To Juanita fell the knowledge that death to the SCLC leader could be a reality and not just a possibility.

During the Memphis march, many people commented on the maturity with which Yoki conducted herself. At the age of twelve, she had the bearing of a fourteen-year-old. Hearts seemed drawn to Marty, who had in recent days traveled some with his father. Marty had believed his dad could cure all of the evils in the country and then would go to other countries to cure the ills there single-handedly. The only other person he believed could possibly help his miracle-man father was his father's best friend, Rev. Abernathy.

While the plane was preparing to land in Memphis, Marty was concerned that the persons who had murdered his father might kill him and the others. Coretta tried to reassure him that police were waiting to protect them.

Perhaps one of the greatest things done for the King children was done that day in Memphis, when they saw their strong mother not give way to hopeless sorrow but respond with the creative act of fulfilling their father's wish for a peaceful march. They saw that his work would be carried on by the thousands who marched with their mother.

Tuesday, April 9, saw the most unusual funeral in the history of the nation. One hundred fifty thousand people attended. It was the largest funeral ever accorded a private citizen in the United States. African Americans, whites, and people of all races attended. Maids, governors, janitors, shoeshine boys, mayors, and millionaires converged on Atlanta. So large was the funeral, offices were set up at the airport with people stationed there around the clock directing people to housing and transportation.

The funeral was planned around three important things in Martin Luther King's life: his church, Ebenezer, where he had grown up; his school, Morehouse College, where he had been an undergraduate; and his work, civil rights, symbolized by a march.

The funeral was held in three parts: First, a funeral at Ebenezer. So many dignitaries attended that there was no seating space for the SCLC staff and families. During a short meeting prior to the funeral, Andrew Young explained the situation. He said it was known from the beginning that the church would be too small, but this was where Dr. King had spent so much of his life. Therefore, this is where the service should be held. He asked the staff members if they would give up their seats for the sake of protocol. There was a great deal of disappointment, but they saw no other way out. Such an unselfish deed, they finally conceded, would be a testament to Dr. King.

Vice President Hubert Humphrey represented the White House. Senator and Mrs. Robert F. Kennedy; Mrs. John F. Kennedy; Governor and Mrs. Nelson Rockefeller of New York; the mayor of New York City, John V. Lindsay; and Michigan's governor, George Romney, were present.

Later Robert Kennedy peeled off his suit coat and, to the delight of thousands, marched and sang in the second part of the funeral, a five-mile march from Ebenezer to Morehouse, where the third part of the funeral was held.

Coretta left Ebenezer riding, but she soon got out of the car and began to walk behind the old weather-beaten wagon drawn by two Georgia brown mules carrying the African wood casket. The cart was to symbolize the humility of King and the Poor People's Campaign in which carts were to be used to carry people to Washington, D.C.

Coretta sat in silence through the church services. She did in life what her husband had done in death and in the movement—tugged at the conscience of America. When would justice come? How many men, women, and children must die?

As important people came and went at the King home that day, the most moving figure was Mrs. John F. Kennedy. Mrs. Kennedy entered the house accompanied by a friend, Rachel Mellon. She paused to sign the guest book and then moved slowly down the hall to Coretta's bedroom, speaking to the King children for a moment. Mrs. Kennedy could perhaps understand Coretta's grief better than anyone else.

Betty Washington, former associate editor of the *Chicago Defender*, described the meeting between the two widows, one black and one white, one with a fresh grief and one with signs of bereavement she had suffered five years earlier: "Mrs. Kennedy stretched out her arms and took the quivering black woman to her breast. Then the two women stood apart." Both Mrs. King and Mrs. Kennedy were dressed in black silk suits. These two women hold a special place with African Americans. With the death of the president, African Americans felt they had lost a trusted friend. Mrs. Kennedy, with her courage and erectness, gave strength to them. Coretta was doing the same thing during this crisis. Courage and faith in God had always been a part of Coretta, but never was the need so great as in this hour.

Coretta's becoming frightened and backing away from the movement when their home was bombed could have caused Dr. King to withdraw from the struggle. She went to his side in Harlem when he was stabbed by a mentally ill woman. She carried on his work while he recuperated. At any time during the struggle, she could have applied wifely pressures for her husband to go slow. After all, with a doctorate he could have had a top position on a safe campus or in a large church. Most likely he would still be alive.

Coretta, perhaps for herself, perhaps for the people, perhaps to ensure that her husband's work would go on, kept a speaking engagement of Martin's at an antiwar rally in New York City's Central Park on her birthday, April 27, 1968.

Coretta began her address with, "I come to New York today with a strong feeling that my dearly beloved husband, who was snatched suddenly from our midst slightly more than three weeks ago now, would have wanted me to be present today. Though my heart is heavy with grief from having suffered an irreparable personal loss, my faith in the redemptive will of God is stronger today than ever before."

She spoke of the many scraps of paper her husband carried, on which he made notes for speeches. Among such notes she had found his "Ten Commandments on Vietnam." She thought perhaps they were to have been delivered as part of his speech at the antiwar rally. Coretta read:

1. Thou shalt not believe in military victory.
2. Thou shalt not believe in political victory.
3. Thou shalt not believe that the Vietnamese love us.
4. Thou shalt not believe that the Saigon government has the support of the people.
5. Thou shalt not believe that the majority of the South Vietnamese look upon the Viet Cong as terrorists.
6. Thou shalt not believe the figures of killed enemies or killed Americans.

7. Thou shalt not believe that the generals know best.
8. Thou shalt not believe that the enemy's victory means communism.
9. Thou shalt not believe the world supports the United States.
10. Thou shalt not kill.

Coretta went on to point out that his major address on Vietnam was on April 4, 1967, and the date he was killed was April 4, 1968. She recalled how troubled he was over the great misunderstanding that had taken place because of his stand. His motives and loyalty to his country had been questioned, but during 1968 there was the possibility that two peace candidates might come out front-runners for the presidency of the United States.

On the flight home from the Memphis march, Coretta had said she intended to keep struggling for rights and peace, and in the coming weeks, months, and years she helped to lead the African American fight for justice.

CHAPTER 10

ON HER OWN

Although 1968 was a sad year for her, people soon realized that Coretta Scott King moved through it with personal strength. Those close to Coretta knew the faith she had in God. Her desire to complete Martin's and her calling kept her focused on the projects Martin had been working on at the time of his death. However, Coretta's greatest concern was her children, and most of her time was devoted to nurturing them. Therefore she carefully chose the projects in which to involve herself personally.

Early in January of 1968, Martin Luther King, Jr., had several meetings with the leaders from the Appalachian white American, Hispanic American, Puerto Rican, Native American, Asian American, and African American communities with the desire of taking America's poor to the nation's capital. Martin hoped that the American people would force Congress to pass legislation to address poverty in America. Martin would name it the Poor People's Campaign. After his death in April of 1968, SCLC workers renamed the Washington campsite Resurrection City.

The Poor People's Campaign was Martin's effort to end poverty in America. Up to that time, the Civil Rights Movement had benefited chiefly the middle class. The right to eat downtown, to travel unhampered, to buy better clothing, and to purchase a house, while important as rights, were still out of the reach of the frustrated poor. What good were these new rights if one did not have the money with which to do these things? King's long-planned campaign was meant to address the underlying issue of poverty.

On May 2, 1968, Coretta launched the march on Washington of the Poor People's Campaign from the Memphis motel balcony where her husband had been shot. She and A.D. King, who was accidentally drowned a year later, unveiled a commemorative plaque, and Coretta spoke: "On this spot where my husband gave his life, I pledge eternal loyalty to the work he so nobly began. His legacy will lead us to the point where all God's children have shoes."

The march was led by a mule-drawn wagon similar to the one that bore King's body through the streets of Atlanta. About a thousand persons marched. Walking at the head of the line were Abernathy, his wife, Juanita, SCLC staff people, Reres Lopez Tüerina, a Mexican-American from New Mexico, and Linda Aranayndo, a Native American. The group marched through the slum area singing "We Shall Overcome," the song of the nonviolent movement, urging others to join the demonstration. The marchers were taunted by several small white groups.

Once at the city limits, the campaign participants boarded buses to take them to Marks, Mississippi, where others would join the caravan and go on to Washington. The campaign was scheduled to begin on May 11, 1968, and end on June 24, 1968. The time was extended one week because a mule wagon arrived late. During that time, poor Americans across the nation were taken to Washington, D.C., by way of bus, mule wagon, and train. One of the largest groups left Chicago via bus. Each city the buses stopped in, an additional bus was added. There were a total of 17 buses when the Chicago group arrived in Washington, D.C.

Coretta made several trips from Atlanta to Washington, D.C., during the Poor People's Campaign. The people named the Poor People's Campaign Children's Daycare the Coretta Scott King Daycare.

Once again, Coretta King introduced Rev. Abernathy as the new leader of the SCLC. Abernathy began the Poor People's Campaign speech with empowering words that united the people from various cities.

The Poor People's Campaign was successful at bringing the plight of poor Americans to the nation's attention. Even today, much can be learned from the campaign's focus and tactics for a new generation of the poor in America to confront the government and the nation with the deep injustice of poverty.

Early in June, Coretta flew to California to comfort Ethel Kennedy on the death of her husband, Robert Kennedy, who was assassinated on the evening he won the California primary. Oddly enough, on the day of Kennedy's funeral, while Coretta sat through the services, she was notified that James Earl Ray, a suspect in the slaying of Martin, had been captured in England.

Later when Ray pleaded guilty, thus eliminating a trial, Coretta expressed that the first reaction of the family was one of relief that they did not have to relive those terrible days again. Whatever the sentence was to be, Coretta, in the spirit of nonviolence, did not want Ray sent to his death.

Amid her loss and anguish, Coretta did not utter a bitter word. She did in fact turn the other cheek.

Coretta did not let grief deter her. During the year following her husband's death, Coretta received an honorary Doctor of Humane Letters degree from Boston University, became the first woman to speak at historic St. Paul's Cathedral in London, and received Yale University's first Frances Blanshard Fellowship Award. In Italy she received the 1969 San Valentian award. She traveled to India and Jamaica to accept awards posthumously for Martin. Coretta went into seclusion in New England to complete her memoirs, *My Life with Martin Luther King, Jr.*, which was published in 1969. A revised edition was released in 1993.

The world saw the faith, desire, and determination Coretta Scott King possessed. She was rated the fifth Most Admired Woman in the World by a 1968 Gallup Poll.

In support of Abernathy and the SCLC, Coretta went to Charleston, South Carolina, in early May 1969 to lead striking members of mostly black local 1199-B of the Drug and Hospital Union. The union was five hundred fifty members, all nonprofessional workers at a state-run Charleston hospital. Most of those striking were woman, licensed practical nurses, nurses' aides, housekeepers, dietary and laundry workers, as well as some male orderlies, food handlers, and attendants.

The city was tense. One thousand National Guard troops patrolled the streets along with four hundred state troopers. The troopers and guardsmen were called in after the city claimed that African Americans rioted and threw rocks through store windows.

Coretta was met by a motorcade of 150 cars at the Charleston airport. She had come on the invitation of the Charleston chapter of the SCLC and was eager to visit Abernathy at the county jail. He was among five hundred African Americans who had been arrested for participating in earlier marches supporting the strikers.

Coretta spent about forty-five minutes with Abernathy and then went to the Emmanuel African Methodist Episcopal Church, where she addressed seven thousand people. Only a third of them could get into the church. The rest listened outside over the loudspeaker system.

Many people were surprised at the African American Charlestonians' emotional response to Coretta. As Coretta had done before, she expressed disappointment at not having gone to jail, explaining her husband had thought their children too young to understand. She said that when she was trying to prepare her children for the fact that she would be going to Charleston and perhaps to jail, Marty had cried, "Now I won't have a mommy or a daddy."

At that time it was apparent that whatever Coretta chose to do, she would have a following. As she led the two-mile march to the Charleston hospital and back to Emmanuel Church, African Americans lined the street. Some of them joined the march. Some tried to touch the hem of her garment. The National Guard troops and state troopers pressed close but were reluctant to arrest her. They watched Coretta kneel on the hot pavement to pray.

CORETTA

A man in Chicago was heard to say that day that he had never participated in any marches, and he had stayed clear of the South, but if Coretta was arrested or mistreated in any way, he was going to Charleston on the first plane he could get. He expressly stated he would not sit still and see Martin Luther King's widow be mistreated!

CHAPTER 11

THE LEGACY

When Martin Luther King, Jr., died in 1968, he was only thirty-nine years old and his widow only thirty-eight. Coretta immediately faced not only a life without her husband and partner and the prospect of raising four small, fatherless children, but also the daunting task of furthering Martin's work and preserving his legacy. Despite her frequent singing at Freedom Concerts, her occasional travel with Martin, and limited public speaking, Coretta had been a very traditional housewife, and her husband's work had not fully utilized her gifts and talents.

Yet all that was to change. If Coretta's journeys back to Memphis and then to New York and Washington, D.C., signaled her intent to carry on Martin's work, subsequent weeks, months, and years amply confirmed it. As she later told Pastor Eddie Long, "I did not just marry a man, I married a destiny."

Coretta saw the need not only to keep alive Martin's work and memory but also to take up the cause in her own right. She did not want to be seen as simply the widow of the slain civil rights leader. As she said four years later, "I must say that I have a strong reaction against being a symbol. . . . You are supposed to grace occasions and you really don't have much to say being the widow of a great man. I embraced the cause just as my husband did, and I would have done so anyway, had I not met Martin."

Coretta's story during the second half of her life was how she managed to raise high the memory of Martin Luther King, Jr., in American life and to create a center for continuing his work. But it was also the story of how she herself emerged as a strong and influential champion of justice in her own right nationally and internationally. As Woodie W. White, retired Methodist bishop and fellow Atlantan observed, "She didn't just carry on his legacy. She carried on the fight against injustice because that was who she was as a person."

But first came family. Coretta's natural stoicism and dignity were in evidence to millions as they watched her on television during the national trauma of her husband's death and funeral. Yet even when she returned to the quiet of their split-level red-brick house on Sunset Avenue in Atlanta, she chose to keep her grief to herself. "I would wake up in the morning, have my cry, then go in to them [the children]," she told *People* magazine. "The children saw me going forward." Aged from five to twelve at the time, the King children retained vivid memories of playing with their father and going swimming and bowling, and playing basketball or football in the yard with him. "Throughout the tragedy," Coretta said, "I tried to observe and give them a kind of feeling about it that would help them. I don't know what I conveyed to them, but I do feel that I've been able to give them a kind of relaxed feeling and an attitude of acceptance, not bitterness."

As their house filled with great bags of mail and condolences, Coretta began to pull together the resources needed to bring up the children, be available for travel, and organize her work. She set up the downstairs offices, once used by Martin, as a place for handling mail. She assembled a small staff to respond to her mail and to start raising money for a center. Meanwhile, the children continued attending Spring Street Elementary School, one of Atlanta's best public schools. Then in 1969 when Yolanda began high school, Coretta enrolled the other children in the Galloway School, a private school ten miles away, to give them more concentrated attention. Despite her hectic life, Coretta was systematic about her children's schooling and extracurricular activities, keeping an organized schedule for each child. Remarkably, life went on.

It must have been strange and perplexing for Coretta's children to deal with their own private feelings about such a public tragedy. And growing up in the shadow of their great father certainly engendered high expectations of them. As Yolanda has said, "To many people, [my father] was a saint, so we were like the saint-ettes." Yet each of the King children has developed his or her own interests and gifts and connected with the King legacy in a distinctive way. Yolanda attended Smith College and nurtured her gifts for acting, directing, and using the performing arts to teach people about issues of justice and rights. She has spoken widely and eloquently on the issues. Dexter Scott graduated from his father's alma mater, Morehouse College, and developed a keen interest in his father's and mother's work. He served as president and CEO of the King Center from 1995 to 2004. Martin Luther King III was also a Morehouse grad, where he majored in political science, and he later worked on voter registration and promotion of the King holiday. Bernice A. King, the youngest, followed her father into the ministry and is a dynamic Atlanta pastor. Perhaps she spoke for all the children in 2001, when she reflected on the struggles, expectations, and inevitable controversies that being a member of the King family would entail. "It is difficult being the daughter of such an awesome man, to be his child and to live with the criticism and the ridicule. . . . Sometimes I feel like backing off and honestly saying to hell with it all. But God has commissioned and commanded that I be true to what he has given me in this great legacy."

After her children and family, Coretta's most piercing dedication was to the King Center, as a means of institution-alizing Martin's concept of social change. There would be no greater test of her resourcefulness and tenacity.

After Martin's death, Coretta presented the SCLC board with a proposal for establishing the Martin Luther King, Jr., Center. The board turned her down. They said Martin would not want a national center named for him. They also believed it would take away funds from the SCLC.

Coretta was hurt by the comments of some of the men who had supported Martin. A disappointed yet determined Coretta went out and established the Martin Luther King, Jr., Center for Nonviolent Social Change on her own. For support Coretta could count on Mayor Ivan Allen, of Atlanta, who had always been supportive of Coretta and her work. To create funding for the center, Coretta turned to entertainers, foundation grants, and major American philanthropists. She also relied on average citizens through fund-raising drives Coretta began doing a great deal of public speaking. Once she started giving speeches in the United States to organizations for the support of nonviolence, the end of racism, and the promotion of human rights, she began receiving speaking requests from around the world.

The popular singer-songwriter Stevie Wonder used his influence to involve other entertainers and to raise money for the center. Stevie Wonder had become an advocate of nonviolence as a means of solving social change across the world. His adamant support brought new attention to the center and its work.

Coretta began work on the Center immediately in 1968 and announced plans in 1969. She initially worked with Dr. Vincent Harding, the esteemed historian from Spelman College, but as time went on and fund-raising and staffing difficulties materialized, plans for the center were modified and focused on a place for the tomb of Martin Luther King, a research center and library, an exhibit area, and a programmatic focus on economic empowerment through militant nonviolent action. Also envisioned was restoration of Martin's boyhood home. In Coretta's mind, the Martin Luther King, Jr., Center for Nonviolent Social Change would be a "research-action center," a place that would gather and coordinate civil rights activities from all around the country. It would emphasize education and training for economic boycotts and other direct nonviolent action tools of the movement.

With grants and contributions, Coretta was able to set up some research functions within the next few years. But because of the steep challenges of raising $8 million, land acquisition, projects for neighborhood restoration, and planning, the center did not officially open until thirteen years later, in 1982.

Today the King Center is a working complex in the heart of the Sweet Auburn residential area, near Martin's boyhood home and the Ebenezer Church he served as copastor. The area has been declared a National Historic Site. At the heart of the center stands the tomb of Dr. King, a marble crypt atop a large reflecting pool that suggests the Prophet Amos's admonition, "Let justice roll down like waters." The pool is surrounded by a covered brick promenade, which leads to Freedom Hall. It is the center's primary exhibit facility, and it includes an auditorium and bookshop, in addition to a foyer filled with art related to Dr. King and to the search for justice. The Freedom Hall complex also houses the center's library and archives. The National Park Service operates a visitor center across the street, where exhibits and video presentations about Dr. King and about children of the movement are shown. The King Center draws 650,000 visitors each year.

As Coretta envisioned from the start, center programs not only honor Dr. King's memory but also promote understanding and practice of the nonviolent methods he espoused for social change. The library is an unparalleled resource for research on the civil rights era, and the center sponsors scholarly and historical work there as well as an annual "summit" on service. The Beloved Community Network and several educational programs coordinate volunteer service projects.

The center is believed to be the first facility in the
United States whose central purpose is teaching Kingian nonviolence. Having earned an undergraduate degree in the field
of education, Coretta developed courses and workshops in
nonviolence taught at the center. Christine King Farris, sister to Martin King and also an educator, produced several
books for grade school students on the principles of Kingian
nonviolence that are also used at the center. One year Coretta
addressed a group of four thousand students on the subject of
nonviolence. She also worked with groups of policemen and
gang members.

Coretta was also intimately involved in the King Papers
Project, an ambitious effort to collate and edit the rich liter-
ary legacy of Dr. King. In 1985 she invited Stanford University historian Clayborne Carson to direct the project, which is
publishing a definitive fourteen-volume edition of Dr. King's
papers, correspondence, sermons, speeches, published writings,
and unpublished manuscripts. Five volumes are already in print.

More broadly, through Coretta's personal involvement and public presence, the King Center has also become a
national catalyst for legislation on civil rights and for voter-
registration campaigns, as well as the for training, encourage-
ment, and development of political leadership among women
and minorities. Despite limited resources, the center's programs
have trained tens of thousands of people in the philosophy and
methods of nonviolence. The center also presents an annual
Martin Luther King Jr. Prize, awarded to such lights as Mrs.
Rosa Parks and President Jimmy Carter.

Probably no single project was closer to Coretta's heart
than the fifteen-year campaign for the creation of Martin

Luther King Day. The first person to suggest the Martin
Luther King, Jr., holiday was Congressman John Conyers of
Detroit, Michigan. For several years he placed a bill before
Congress to create a holiday in Dr. King's name.

Even before a holiday was set aside by legislation, Americans recalled Martin Luther King in several ways. On his
birthday, schools, churches, and communities observed the day
with memorials, workshops, seminars, city-wide services, and
parades.

Americans knew Martin lost his life fighting for human
rights and making America a more democratic nation. They
knew the Civil Rights Act of 1964 and the Voting Rights
Acts of 1965 were products of Martin Luther King, Jr.'s work.
The Civil Rights Act of 1964 guaranteed equal use of public accommodations, and the Voting Rights Act put an end to
poll taxes, the use of examinations and reprisals used to keep
African Americans and the poor from voting. No one was hap-
pier than Coretta on Wednesday, October 19, 1983. On that
day the Senate passed the King Holiday Bill 78 to 22. This
made the third Monday of January a legal holiday honoring
Dr. Martin Luther King, Jr. As a part of the celebration of the
momentous event, President Ronald Reagan and Mrs. Coretta
Scott King hosted approximately 350 people two weeks later
at the signing of the Holiday Bill in the historic United States
Capitol rose garden.

During the event President Ronald Reagan, who had
originally opposed the holiday idea, praised it and said, "Each
year on Martin Luther King, Jr., Day let us not only recall
Dr. King, but rededicate ourselves to the commandments he

believed in and sought to live every day—'Thou shalt love thy God with all thy heart and thou shalt love thy neighbor as thyself.'" Coretta Scott King told the audience: "America is a more democratic nation, a more just nation, a more peaceful nation because Martin Luther King, Jr., became the preeminent nonviolent commander."

Coretta was credited with creating and keeping an atmosphere that caused Americans not to forget the focus of a national holiday for Martin. Those close to Coretta knew that without her hard work, lobbying, and persistence, the bill would not have passed. They jokingly referred to it as "Coretta's Holiday Bill."

Coretta did not want the holiday to represent a day for commercial sales and buying, nor just another day off of work. She wanted the holiday to represent a day for all Americans to be on the task of serving humanity, for which Martin worked. Coretta wanted it to be a day when Americans would work toward keeping Martin's dream and legacy alive. She chaired a commission that formalized plans for the annual celebration, which began in January 1986. It took another full decade of work by Coretta and others to ensure that the holiday was honored by each of the states.

As the 1970s and 1980s were spent building the King legacy, the 1990s saw Coretta and her family focused more on preserving it. Disposition of Dr. King's papers led to controversy for Coretta. In 1987 she sued Boston University, demanding that the school relinquish 83,000 documents that Dr. King had deposited at the university four years before he was murdered. She maintained that it was never Martin's plan to leave the papers there. After six years of legal wrangling, the case finally went to trial in Boston and was ultimately unsuccessful.

A similar five-year controversy erupted when the King estate challenged the right of national broadcaster CBS to use and license its footage of the 1963 March on Washington and Dr. King's speech there. While neither the network nor the estate ever backed down, in July 2000 the estate agreed to drop its lawsuit in exchange for an undisclosed payment and use of the film for its own productions.

The constant tension between the center's two missions—preserving the memory of Dr. King and furthering the work of nonviolent social change—posed tough choices with limited resources and led sometimes to disagreements even within the family over the center's future.

CHAPTER 12

CHAMPION OF JUSTICE

The world into which Coretta Scott King thrust herself after Martin's death was markedly different than the one they had faced together in Montgomery. This was in part because historic court cases and legislation mandated the rights that the movement had long sought for African Americans. But the United States was deeply embroiled in the Vietnam War, a conflict that took black lives disproportionately and robbed the government of resources to address poverty and related issues. Growing discontent among African Americans, which erupted in America's cities after his assassination, burned away the hard-won consensus about their best strategy. New movements of liberation around the world and among other minority groups pressed for attention.

As she stepped out on her own, Coretta brought a clear and unwavering vision for justice to an often conflicting and bewildering scene. Though always bound intimately to Martin's cause, her commitments were authentically her own. She often noted her own formative experiences in childhood and college, saying, "It was my cause before I ever met him." In countless travels, speeches, and conferences over the next thirty-five years after his death, the first lady of Civil Rights supported struggles everywhere against what she dubbed the triple evils of racism, poverty, and war.

It was not easy. In the early days of the movement, she had not often spoken publicly. But even with her first speech, in 1958, "I felt from that experience, you know, that God had intended me to sing, but you know, I'm not sure, maybe He wants me to speak, too." When sometimes Martin would balk at her public appearances, she told him that she shared his call. "Can't you understand?" she asked. "You know I have an urge to serve just like you have."

Coretta quickly began to bring her notability and standing to bear on the issues that meant most to her: jobs, discrimination and affirmative action, military spending, and, later, gender justice, AIDS education, and gun violence. She leaped into the presidential contest of 1972 with an endorsement of George McGovern and thereafter was sought out by candidates at all levels for endorsement and support.

Despite its unpopularity, she continued Martin's strong stand against the war in Vietnam, and later, during the administration of Ronald Reagan, spoke out strongly against the military buildup and nuclear-arms race. Opposed to both wars in the Persian Gulf, Coretta used her Martin Luther King Day message in 1991 to call for a cease-fire in that conflict. She saw an intimate connection between militarism and economic injustice, and between sexism and militarism. She was especially active in the National Organization for Women, the Women's International League for Peace, and Church Women United.

Coretta saw military spending in part as robbing other priorities, especially education. As she noted in 1991, "The U.S. is spending 55 cents out of every taxpayer dollar on the military, compared to just 2 cents for education." Held hostage by that funding "are American school children, the nation's 3 million homeless people, the 20 million Americans who experience hunger every day, and the 37 million Americans who have no health insurance." It was her conviction, she said, that "we cannot eradicate illiteracy and other social problems until we eradicate the scourges of militarism from the face of the earth."

Jobs were always a priority for Coretta. She took such initiatives as setting up in the mid-1970s a Full Employment Action Council at the center, with herself as president, to push for political action on the continuing high levels of unemployment in the African American community. She was a strong supporter of the Humphrey-Hawkins Full-Employment Act of 1978.

Jobs and justice were also behind Coretta's strong support of affirmative action programs, which attempted to redress the historic lack of opportunities in jobs and education for African Americans and other minorities. She fought against a California initiative attacking affirmative action, writing, "Like my husband, I strongly believe that affirmative action has merit, not only for promoting justice, but also for healing and unifying society." In 1977 she joined other civil rights leaders and groups in urging federal action in favor of affirmative action in light of the court challenge to it from white California law-school applicant Allan Bakke.

Coretta's continued advocacy for human rights led to an annual "State of the Dream" speech she delivered at the center, in which she offered a domestic and international survey of gains and challenges to human rights and democratic governance.

Her international travels were extensive, and she joined Andrew Young as a member of the U.S. delegation to the UN general Assembly in 1977.

With Yolanda by her side, she also organized protests in 1985 of Apartheid outside the South African embassy in Washington, D.C. Yet her 1986 trip to South Africa proved controversial because of her plans to meet with the head of state, President Pieter W. Botha and Zulu leader Mangosuthu Buthelezi. Under pressure she canceled those meetings at the last minute in favor of a visit to Soweto and meetings with Mrs. Nelson Mandela and activist Allan Boesak. Coretta described her meeting with Winnie Mandela, wife of the long-jailed Nelson Mandela, as "one of the greatest and most meaningful moments of my life." She also was escorted by newly installed Archbishop Desmond Tutu on a visit to Apartheid-enforced squatter camps. Ten years later she stood with Mandela as he was sworn in as president of South Africa.

Coretta also courted controversy but was typically unwavering in her support of full rights for gays and lesbians, saying in a November 2000 speech, "I appeal to everyone who believes in Martin Luther King Jr.'s dream to make room at the table of brotherhood and sisterhood for lesbian and gay people." The breadth of her vision of human rights earned her honors from the American Bar Association in 2004, which noted that "she carried the message of peace, nonviolence, and the need to work against injustice to several continents and to all corners of the United States." At one time several people asked her to fire a gay employee due to his sexual orientation. Coretta refused; she said that he had always done a great job and that everyone deserved to work.

Coretta spoke often and insistently for the exoneration of James Earl Ray, who had confessed to murdering Dr. King, then recanted. Coretta and others in her family believed that Ray had been framed and that her husband's murder was perhaps part of a larger plot, perhaps even involving the government. In April 1998 she recommended that a "Truth and Reconciliation Commission" be established to find out what was behind the killing. Although unpopular, her persistence had a further point about the deeper meaning of racial violence in America. "I realize," she said then, "that many people would rather forget about the assassination of my husband, and for America to focus on working toward the goals that defined his dream for America. But I feel strongly that you can't heal the scars of racial violence without exposing them to the light of truth." Still, after a Department of Justice investigation, prosecutors found no credible evidence of a conspiracy that involved or used Ray in the killing.

Although Coretta participated in numberless demonstrations and protests, from a massive May 1969 demonstration in Charleston, South Carolina, in support of striking hospital workers, through a rally and march supporting busing in Boston in 1974, to her arrest at the 1985 protests of Apartheid, probably no demonstrations were closer to her heart than the two commemorations, in 1983 and 2003, of the 1963 March on Washington for Jobs and Freedom, in the course of which Martin had given his most famous speech.

In 1983 she led an effort that brought eight hundred human rights organizations—the Coalition of Conscience—and a half-million demonstrators to Washington, D.C., to remember but also to urge more government involvement in the plight of the poor. Twenty years later she joined a much smaller group, numbering in the thousands, for an emotional and spirited reunion that unveiled a marker commemorating the speech. But the weekend's festivities also reflected the broadening of civil rights constituencies. It included not only Coretta and the King family and such stalwarts of the movement as the Reverend Jesse Jackson, former congressman John Lewis, and D.C. congressional delegate Eleanor Holmes Norton, but also Arab Americans, Hispanics, gays and lesbians, and other groups more newly alert to the cause and the ongoing campaign for social justice.

As Coretta approached her seventy-fifth year, she could reflect back on her journey with pride. "I would like to think that my years of working for peace, human rights, and a society free of racism, sexism, homophobia and all forms of bigotry have helped to make life a little better for your generation," she said at Bennett College in 2002. Two years later she returned to Boston, where she had first met Martin. Coming full circle, she had traveled to receive an outstanding alumna award from her alma mater, the New England Conservatory of Music. How differently everything had turned out from what she could have envisioned fifty years earlier! Yet through it all and in the end, Coretta Scott King had truly found her voice.

FOR FURTHER READING

Lewis V. Baldwin. *There Is a Balm in Gilead: The Cultural Roots of Martin Luther King, Jr.* Minneapolis: Fortress Press, 1991.

Lewis V. Baldwin. *To Make the Wounded Whole: The Cultural Legacy of Martin Luther King, Jr.* Minneapolis: Fortress Press, 1992.

Taylor Branch. *Parting the Waters: America in the King Years, 1954–63.* New York: Simon & Schuster, 1988.

Taylor Branch. *Pillar of Fire: America in the King Years, 1963–65.* New York: Simon & Schuster, 1998.

David J. Garrow. *Bearing the Cross: Martin Luther King, Jr., and the Southern Christian Leadership Conference.* New York: Vintage, 1988.

Coretta Scott King. *My Life with Martin Luther King, Jr.* New York: Henry Holt, 1993.

Martin Luther King, Jr. *Stride toward Freedom.* New York: Harper, 1964.

Martin Luther King, Jr. *The Measure of a Man.* Facets. Minneapolis: Fortress Press, 2001.

Martin Luther King, Jr. *Strength to Love.* Philadelphia: Fortress Press, 1981.

Rosetta E. Ross. *Witnessing and Testifying: Black Women, Religion, and Civil Rights.* Minneapolis: Fortress Press, 2003.